Lessons from History

Reflections on the past, Present & Future of Two Muslim communities

Dr Israr Ahmad

Istinarah Press

2023 CE – 1444 H

It should be perfectly clear that the Qur'ān is only authentic in its original language, Arabic. Since perfect translation of the Qur'ān is impossible, we have used the translation of the meaning of the Qur'ān throughout the book, as the result is only a crude meaning of the Arabic text.

Qur'ānic verses appear in speech marks proceeded by a reference to the Surah and verse number. Sayings (*Hadith*) of Prophet Muhammad ρ appear in inverted commas along with reference to the Hadith Book and its Reporter.

Contents

Foreword

The substance of this book is based on the ideas published by Dr. Israr Ahmad in 1993 in the columns of the Urdu daily *Nawa-e-Waqt* of Lahore. The series of write-ups continued for a few months and were widely read with interest. The entire material, after slight editing, was published in a book form in October 1993 under the *title Sabiqa aur Maujuda Musalman Ummatun ka Mazi, Haal, aur Mustaqbil,* and has since gone through many re-prints. Dr. Ahmed Afzaal rendered these ideas into English and part of it was serialized in 1995-96 in the monthly *Hikmat-e-Qur'an* published by the Markazi Anjuman Khuddam-ul-Qur'an Lahore. For putting it into a compact book, he further revised the entire material, added his own sub-titles, and made it more authentic by giving quotations from the Old and New Testaments. Indeed, he took great pains to make the citations of quite a few historical events and landmarks, particularly of early Jewish history, more authentic by giving dates and references from reliable sources. Moreover, he suggested a much more telling title for the book — *Lessons from History* — and the sub-title — *Reflections on the Past, Present, and Future of Two Muslim Communities* — puts in a capsule form the whole spectrum of ideas covered in the book.

Dr. Israr Ahmad, as a true believer, is absolutely convinced of the indivisibility and essential identity of the Messages of all prophets. All Scriptures stem from and are parts of a single Source, the *Mother of Books* and the *Hidden Book*. According to the Qur'an, Prophethood is indeed an indivisible office: one cannot believe in some and not in others without *giving the lie* to the very source of Revelation. From the very beginning of the prophetic career, Prophet Muhammad (saw) was himself absolutely convinced of the Divine character of the earlier revealed documents and the

Divine Messengership of the bearers of those documents. This is why he recognized without a moment of hesitation that Abraham, Moses, Jesus, and other Old and New Testament religious personalities had been genuine prophets like himself. Thus the true followers of Moses were, according to the Qur'an, also Muslims as were the true followers of Prophet Jesus, until they deviated from the Right Path and adopted certain beliefs central to their creeds. The most important of these are the Jewish claim to election and equally exclusivist claims to truth adopted by Christians. The Qur'anic assertion in the unity and universality of Divine Guidance and the proclamation that Allah (swt) had left no nation or people on earth without sending guidance to them directly ran counter to these claims. (For example Surah Al- Fatir 35:24.) Further "*neither Jews nor Christians will be happy with you until you follow their religion; Say, Guidance is God's Guidance*" (Al-Baqarah 2:111). And again, "Jews say, Christians have nothing to stand on, and Christians say, Jews have nothing to stand on — while both recite the (same) Books" (Al-Baqarah 2:113). It is true that between Jews and Christians, the Qur'an prefers the latter as we read: "*Among them there are priests and monks and they are not a conceited people*" (Al-Ma'ida 5:82), and "*We cast in the hearts of his (Jesus') followers kindness and mercy*" (Al- Hadeed 57:27). Nevertheless, Christians' belief in incarnation and Trinity is castigated in the severest terms throughout the Qur'an.

The ultimate outcome of this line of thought is the eventual religious disassociation of the prophets of these two communities — particularly those of the Jews — from their followers. "*Abraham was neither Jew nor Christians, but an undeviating monotheist and Muslim*" (Aal-e-Imran 2:67). "They say, '*Become Jews or Christians, you will find right guidance.' Say, 'Rather the religion of Abraham, the non-sectarian, non-deviant monotheist.'*" (Al-Baqarah 2:140). The entire line of Biblical personages is then claimed for Islam, "Say (O Muslims!) 'We believe in God and in what has been sent down to us (i.e., the Qur'an), and what was sent down to Abraham, Ishmael, Isaac, Jacob, and the tribes, and what was given to Moses and to Jesus and what was given to the prophets from their Lord. We set no partition between any of them and we surrender ourselves to God.' If then, Jews and Christians believe as you believe, they are on the right path, but if they turn their back, they are in a wide divergence among themselves...." (Al-Baqarah 2:136,37). It is in light of these Qur'anic teachings that Dr. Israr Ahmad speaks of Bani Israel — the true and non-deviant followers of the Guidance given to Prophet Moses until the advent of Prophet Muhammad (saw) — as the former Muslim *Ummah*. Indeed, according to the Qur'an, there has been only one true religion throughout human history, i.e., Islam; all other systems of belief and worship, as they exist today are nothing but corrupted and distorted versions of the originally pure and *fitric* teachings of various Messengers of God. However, from the standpoint of detailed law (i.e., Shari 'ah), Qur'an clearly regards Bani Israel an *Ummah* distinct from the *Ummah* of Prophet Muhammad (saw) and the change of *Qibla* has a great symbolic significance in this.

For the committed and convinced Muslim, neither the flow of history itself nor the study and interpretation of it can be considered apart from the realm of the sacred and the workings of the Divine. God as Creator is also the Maker of history; His Hand controls every moment in time, every historical event. History is the arena in which His Will is made manifest, His Dominion is expressed, and His Commitment to the fulfillment of its Divinely ordained rules is evidenced.

And yet, in the Islamic understanding, it is not God alone who is responsible for the historical process. Every individual shares in the responsibility insofar as he has assumed through his heritage and according to the verification of the Qur'an a part of the God-given legacy to be a vicegerent, to represent the Divine Will on earth. That role which the Jews and Christians relinquished by veering away from the true worship of the one God is assumed by Muslims as their full and final responsibility. Islam thus bears the obligation to make known to the world the reality of the historical revelation of the Qur'an, that which provides for the proper understanding of God's continuing action in history. Thus the claim of the immutability of "historical laws" — a tenet of the Marxist dogma — cannot subsume the historicity of the Ummah. Islamic faith — the Deen of transcendent norms and values — cannot be interiorized to the extent that Muslim history becomes nothing but a quest for some meta-historical salvation. Neither can the dictates of the Islamic faith be sacrificed at the alter of some unproven and whimsical set of "historical laws." It is so because history for a Muslim is not only a search for theoretical meaning but a spur for practical action as well. His faith dictates that the process of history be subdued to the Will of Allah. To be part of the historical process is to be aware and to be active, bearing fully the responsibility placed on man by his Creator.

Islam exhorts the Muslim to see not only the outward manifestations of the different happenings of the human life, but to study the undercurrent of ideals and motives which have shaped those happenings. The historical references and the accounts of the past events are given in the Qur'an, not so much to fill in the gaps of our factual knowledge, but to systematize and generalize it and to take lessons from it. The Holy Qur'an treats the events of the past not only with a view of reviving them in our memory but for making them meaningful and instructive to us. It selects the significant events, interprets them in the light of moral laws, and then evaluates them according to ethical judgments; and in the whole process of selecting, interpreting, and evaluating the facts it provides answers to the crucial questions about the destiny of mankind. The attitude of Islam towards historical knowledge of different civilizations and cultures is of great significance in human understanding. The Muslim historians generally not only kept the high ideal of objectivity and exactitude in surveying the entire course of human development, but they also sought to determine its origin and goal as well.

The Holy Qur'an and the Hadith urge us to review the past events, both reported and experienced, as indications that they should awaken in us a strong moral sense and at the same time enhance its ability to act according to the commands of God, to penetrate into the apparently meaningless succession of events and discern the ever-present Design and Will of the Creator and perceive that all being and happening in the world is the outcome of a conscious, all- embracing Power, and unless one is in spiritual accord with the demands of that Power, one cannot fulfill the Divine purpose for which he has been sent to this world. It is not without a purpose that God gives dominance to certain people at one time, and deprives them of this position at another occasion. This ebb and rise of the people has a Divine purpose to serve. Thus Qur'an observes: "If a wound has afflicted you, a wound like it also afflicted the disbelieving people, and We bring these days to men by turn, that Allah may know those who believe and take witnesses from among you and Allah loves not the wrong-doers" (Aal-e-Imran 3:140).

Histories of the Jews and the Muslims, being typically woven around Divine Revelation, should provide a Muslim scholar ground for a thoughtful and perceptive comparative study of them. Though in the present day political climate, Jews and Muslims form two totally divergent peoples, yet striking similarities in their temporal histories are found and pointed out in this book. In particular, there is a strong parallelism regarding the two phases of rise and decline experienced by the two religious fraternities during the long course of their histories thus proving literally a tradition of the Holy Prophet (saw) on this subject reproduced in this book.

The view of history in the Muslim mind is, and should be, a prophetic one. In the Qur'an over and over again the historic sequence is repeated — a warning, followed by either repentance or destruction, as God sends His messengers to one nation after another. The Qur'an provides a basis for a moral interpretation of history. The course of history is a moral agency through which the morally superior elements rise to the top, while those who are morally inferior sink to the bottom. That virtuous living, which is the outcome of a healthy religious faith, must inevitably lead to success. This interpretation is deeper and broader than that of Karl Marx because it covers both the moral and material aspects, while that of Marx concentrates entirely on the material aspects, being greatly influenced by the materialistic evolutionary philosophies of his time. Religion is definitely not opium for the people. The impulse towards social emancipation is surely found in Islam. It always aimed at a society where equality, justice, and prosperity would prevail. Islam teaches that God is concerned not only with moral and spiritual life of man but also with total emancipation, justice, and betterment of economic conditions. The Holy Prophet (saw) left for us not only a theory that is preached, but also concrete experience and historical facts.

In the last part of the book, Dr. Israr Ahmad with reference to the predictions of the Holy Prophet Muhammad (saw) reported in authentic traditions, discusses the events which will take place prior to the Doomsday. He is convinced that the global happenings are already moving in that direction. In the Middle East the stage is gradually being set for an ultimate World War between the forces of Good and Evil. Even though in the hard facts prevailing today we generally see a state of humiliation of Muslims and their virtual enslavement by the forces of the New World Order, the author — on the basis of authentic prophetic traditions — has a staunch belief in global domination of Islam. One notes with dismay that very few Islamic scholars nowadays pay heed to these authentic prophecies, according to which four major episodes will take place before the end of the world. In chronological sequence they are as follows:

1. the ultimate World War (*Al-Malhama*) of human history, which will be fought predominantly in the Middle East;
2. the appearance of Anti-Christ, or Dajjal, in the final phase of that War — a leader of the evil forces who will inflict great sufferings and destruction on the Arab Muslims;
3. the re-appearance of Prophet Jesus Christ (AS), who will cause the extermination of Dajjal and his Jewish followers; and finally,
4. the establishment of the System of *Khilafah*, or the domination of Islam, over the entire globe.

The world order as Pax Islamica will be an order of peace where no ethnic group, nation, or religious community would be in conflict with another. Even though it will be an era of the ascendancy of Islam as a socio-political order, individuals will be allowed to adhere to their particular religious beliefs.

The most significant point of Dr. Israr Ahmad's presentation is that he considers the future Muslim leader in the person of "Mehdi" and the re-appearance of Prophet Jesus Christ (AS) — beliefs generally dubbed by modernist Muslims as *Messianic* ideas — to be not only based on genuine and authentic *Ahadith*, but also quite rational and logical implications of the Qur'anic asseverations with regard to Islam's global domination. The noteworthy point in this context, however, is that despite these beliefs his view of Islam is thoroughly dynamic and active. The prophecies of the Prophet (saw) in respect of Islam's domination do not absolve Muslims of discharging their religious obligations in the right earnest. Only true belief, i.e., Iman, and maximum possible effort in the way of Allah (swt) guarantee salvation and eternal bliss in the Hereafter.

Absar Ahmad

Prologue

Anyone who seriously reads newspapers and regularly watches international news would agree that we are living in an age of unprecedented swiftness. Things are changing everywhere with a brisk pace and events are unfolding with an urgent rush. Different characters are entering and exiting the world stage in rapid succession. Each act of the global drama is instantaneously merging with the next. Simultaneously, our daily lives have also undergone an unprecedented acceleration.

Due to all this celerity, most of us are either unable to connect different world events and appreciate their significance, or we are so wrapped up in our own immediate problems that we have simply no time left to brood over international affairs. But our inability to comprehend the global scenario — or our total naïveté concerning the changes at the international level — does not, of course, diminish the importance of these events in any way or obviate the need to study them deeply by placing them in their historical setting. We must remain in touch with the socio-political developments in the world, as ignorance can often lead to extinction.

Traveling Through Time

Let us begin by reflecting on the past and present of the Muslim *Ummah*: her quandaries and dilemmas, her swinging fortunes, her glorious and at times pathetic history, her uncertain present, and, finally, her unknown destiny.

Every concerned and thoughtful Muslim is sure to ponder, at one time or another, over the question of our bewildering rise to politico-economic prominence and then the tragic and deplorable decline. Every historian — whether Muslim or non- Muslim — has his own theory to explain the ups and downs in our fourteen hundred years odyssey. We Muslims, however, are a unique group of people, radically different from all other nations, races, or communities in our very essence. (Our only resemblance, in certain respects, is with the Jews, as we shall discuss later.) This implies that the factors which usually cause rise and decline among other cultures are often not relevant for, or applicable to, the Muslims of the world.

Therefore, in order to make sense of all that is happening to the Muslims throughout the world, it is imperative that we investigate our history very carefully. We must pinpoint the decisive element in *our* rise and fall. We must identify the law that is governing *our* ups and downs. We must analyze our history because the threads of the past are closely linked with those of the future. History, as we keep hearing, repeats itself. By probing the past we may be able to get a vision of the shape of things to come. By examining our history, we may be able to catch a glimpse of our future. Moreover, it is clear that we can chart our future course of action, prudently and wisely, only when we know the path which has led to the present.

The Humiliated Ummah

As for the present condition of Muslims, there are unfortunately few things to boast about. For all practical purposes, the Muslim *Ummah* as an integrated global entity does not exist anywhere in the real world. The authentic and genuine "*Ummah*" has long been reduced to a mere academic concept. In reality, we are left with a large number of Muslim "nations" and their respective "nation-states." We are further divided into even smaller linguistic, racial, and sectarian groups — along with inevitable hostilities and conflicts. The inescapable result has been that although we are at least 1300 million in number, our combined weight in the global policy making process is never more than zero.

It is indeed amazing that we are so many, yet we count for so little. All international disputes are being decided today by the United States and her allies, especially Britain and France, under cover of the UN Security Council. Our national policies — interior, foreign, and fiscal — are being formulated and dictated by the guardians of the New World order, by means of such organizations as the World Bank and the International Monetary Fund. Our natural resources are being controlled and exploited by them. The wealth belonging to most of the affluent Muslim countries is practically at their disposal; as a matter of fact, Western powers can "freeze" this wealth as soon as the country in question attempts to take any step which is opposed to their wishes. The Arab monarchies — despite material prosperity, majestic palaces, and luxurious life style — are nothing but puppets in their hands. Muslim rulers all over the Islamic world are desperately vying to win favors from the West; the interests of Islam and Muslims hardly ever bother them. Most of the Muslim world is dressed in the garb of fear and hunger, and disharmony, disunity, poverty, mediocrity, mismanagement, and corruption are reigning supreme. Even in countries where there is some material prosperity, the ubiquitous humiliation — in the form of disgrace on a global level and lack of genuine autonomy — is still there, as exemplified by the fact that the richest of the Arab Sheikhs are a common laughingstock of Western media.

On top of this, there are the massacres and other forms of sufferings being endured by Muslims in India, Kashmir, Palestine, and elsewhere. The brutalities committed against the Bosnian Muslims are still fresh in our memories. The anguish of hearing how our sisters were raped by the thousands and how our brothers were mercilessly tortured and slained is not something that we can easily forget. To add insult to injury, and much to the satisfaction of our enemies, there are Muslims who kill — or conspire with non- Muslims to suppress — other Muslims, and are often proud of their "achievements."

Who can deny that we are, indeed, a disgraced and dishonored community in the comity of nations?

Going through the Qur'an, we often come across words of severe condemnation which specifically berate the Jews for their sins. We tend to pass over these verses with a smug self-righteousness, satisfied that these admonitions are meant for a corrupt people and that these words have nothing to do with us. But consider the following Qur'anic words with an open mind and an objective attitude, and it would not be difficult to see that, much more than the Jews, these Divine words are actually applicable to the Muslims of today :

Humiliation and misery were stamped upon them, and they drew upon themselves the anger of Allah. (Al-Baqarah 2: 61)

Isn't it a fact that our politics today is nothing but an ignominious slavery to the West? That our economy is based upon nothing but shameful mendicancy? That we are, on the whole, the most ignorant, undisciplined, corrupt, and uncivilized people on the surface of earth? Isn't it true that we are intellectually effete and academically dependent on the West? That we are willing and even eager to collaborate with the enemy so that we may kill our brothers? If all this doesn't constitute the worst form of humiliation, then what does?

A common Muslim may plead before Almighty God: Aren't we supposed to be the best of communities? Aren't we among the followers of your most beloved Prophet (saw)? Aren't the Christians and the Jews and the rest of them enemies of Islam? Then how can anyone justify their domination and opulence and our miseries and destitution?

This most disturbing of questions demands our deepest attention, especially because of the following two reasons:

First, it is imperative that we familiarize ourselves with the Divine Law that has been operating throughout human history. We must understand that instead of being innocent victims of the vagaries of fate, we ourselves are responsible for our pathetic state of existence. We need to clearly realize that mere grumbling and complaining will not solve our problems, and that we need to confess our sins and repent with the true spirit of repentance.

Secondly, just as a correct diagnosis is an indispensable prerequisite for proper treatment, in the same way we need to identify the real cause of our miseries before we can formulate and chart a plan of action. This is important so that the limited amount of energies and resources available to us are not lost in superficial and useless undertakings. Instead, a precise appreciation of the seriousness of our situation, and a correct interpretation of that situation in terms of its etiology — both are essential steps as far as any hopes for a successful revival are concerned.

History is the Key

Before discussing the Divine Law which deals with the rise and fall of nations, civilizations, and empires, it is necessary to emphasize that Almighty Allah (swt) is never a passive onlooker vis-à-vis human history, but that each and every event takes place as a manifestation of His omnipotence and infinite wisdom.

There was an interesting idea called Deism that became popular in the 17th century Europe, the subtle remains of which are still lurking deep down in our minds. According to this view, God did create the universe, but He has long since removed Himself from its affairs, and only the blind and deaf laws of nature are now running the show. God is busy, so to speak, in a sort of self-contemplation, and He doesn't care at all about the humanity He once created.

The Islamic perspective, in sharp contrast to Deism, is that Almighty Allah (swt) is not only the Creator, Designer, and Fashioner of the cosmos, but He is also its Sovereign, Ruler, Administrator, and Guardian. The logical conclusion that necessarily follows from this belief is that nothing happens in the universe — not even the movement of a tiny leaf in the morning breeze — without the permission of Almighty Allah (swt). Although human beings enjoy a limited freedom of action and are, therefore, responsible for the consequences of their actions on the overall historical process, the fact remains that a human action as such is not effective in causing any event, unless it is allowed by Almighty Allah (swt).

Since Almighty Allah (swt) — in addition to being All-Powerful — is also the Most Wise, everything that takes place in the arena of human history has a profound reason which may or may not be immediately apparent to us. Human beings are extremely myopic creatures, lacking the infinitely broad perspective, in terms of both time and space, that is required to appreciate the wisdom and the long-term planning of the Creator. However, with the help of the Holy Qur'an and the guidance provided by Prophet Muhammad (saw), it is possible to understand the general purpose and direction of history in an overall manner, although the meaning behind every individual event and its significance in the Divine scheme will probably remain elusive.

The Holy Qur'an urges us to contemplate the events of the past, as they are indicators of the *sunnah* of Almighty Allah (swt); it teaches us to try and penetrate into the apparently meaningless succession of historical happenings and to discern the design and will of the Creator behind them, and to try and appreciate how the events in the world actually represent the plans of an Omnipotent Supreme Being.

It is important to keep this fact in mind: However random and aimless the events of history may appear, there is a definite purpose behind each one of them. It is the Divine Creative Energy, or the Will of Almighty Allah (swt), that is active in the entire sweep of history. There is a certain order and pattern hidden beneath the plethora of seemingly inconsequential and disconnected historical facts. Nothing is useless, no event is arbitrary or futile. In fact, as we shall see in the later part of this book, a profoundly meaningful evolutionary process is taking place by which humanity is moving, slowly but steadily, toward its final destination. Although the details and finer points of this ongoing process are beyond the reach of human understanding, its broad outline is quite comprehensible.

Within this general scheme of things, there are certain universal truths which remain constant. As the Qur'an warns us:

You will not find any change in the law of God [TMQ Al-Fath 48:23]

The Islamic view of history can be explained in terms of the philosophy of *ideals*, as presented by late Dr. Muhammad Rafiuddin (1904-1969), former director of Iqbal Academy (Karachi, Pakistan). According to him, the unchanging characteristic of the human nature — ingrained, of course, by Almighty Allah (saw) — is that the motivating force behind all human endeavors is the urge for *ideals*. Thus, different stages of the life of a culture-civilization, i.e., birth, growth, decline, and death, can be correctly understood only in terms of this philosophy of *ideals*, briefly described in the following paragraphs.

A number of individuals inspired by a single ideal organize themselves in the form of an ideal-group, e.g. a primitive tribe or a modern state. Their ideal may be a certain personality, a supernatural belief, or a social theory. By definition, members of the ideal-group believe their ideal to be the highest possible form of Beauty and Perfection. They make an effort to realize the ideal in practice, the result of their effort being the intellectual, cultural, and behavioral framework of that particular culture-civilization, including their language, religion, art, music, poetry, architecture, morality, philosophy, science, and law.

Initially, Almighty Allah (swt) allows the culture-civilization to freely prosper and develop in all directions. In due course of time, however, the inherent defects and internal conflicts of the wrong ideal start manifesting and the ideal-group begins to deteriorate. Ultimately, over a variable period of time, the culture- civilization gradually dies and disappears, making way for the next and possibly better ideal to capture the imagination and passion of a fresh generation, and the process repeats itself on a relatively higher plane of evolution. One Qur'anic verse summarizes this entire process in these words:

Do they not see how many generations We did destroy before them, whom We had firmly established in the land as We have not established you, and showered abundant rain on them, and made rivers lap at their feat, yet whom We destroyed for their sins, and raised new generations after them?

[TMQ Al-An'aam 6:6]

A deep study of history will show that the social evolution of humanity is progressing in a particular direction. Adopting and discarding one ideal after another, it is destined to reach the ultimate, permanent, and stable culture-civilization which will be based on the Right Ideal, i.e., an ideal which is in harmony with the human nature, and therefore free from all possible defects. This culture-civilization of the future will be characterized by the domination of the Right Ideal; in other words, by the domination of Islam. We shall return to this topic later in this treatise.

The Wrath of Almighty Allah (swt)

As far as the individual human being is concerned, the Holy Qur'an makes it very clear that the life of this world is only a trial and a test, and that the consequences of good or bad deeds — in the form of rewards or punishments — are reserved for the life-beyond-death, the Hereafter, or the *Al-Aakhira.* Thus, the Almighty says:

Glorious is He who holds the Kingship in His hand, who has power over every thing, who created death and life in order to try you, to see who of you are best of deed. He is All-mighty and Forgiving. [TMQ Al- Mulk 67:1,2]

Verily We created man from a sperm joined (to the ovum) to try him, then gave him hearing and sight. We surely showed him the way that he may either be grateful or deny" [TMQ Al-Dahr 76:2-3]

We have made whatever exists on the earth its adornment to test and try them (and) know who acts better, for We shall certainly turn it to barren dust.

[TMQ Al-Kahf 18:7-8]

This implies that the pains or troubles a person may face during the course of this-worldly life are *not* the penalties or punishments for his wrongdoing; similarly, the material comforts or prosperity or power one may enjoy are similarly *not* the rewards or compensations for his good deeds. What we experience in this life are the different ways in which the Lord tries us. This has been made clear in the Holy Qur'an thus:

Every soul will know the taste of death. We tempt you with evil and with good as a trial; and to Us you will return. [TMQ Al-Anbia 21:35]

However, the most significant point to note is that the above discussion applies only to individuals and not to nations or communities. The Holy

Qur'an teaches us that the manner in which Almighty Allah (swt) deals with different nations is quite different from the way in which He deals with individual human beings. The rewards and punishments for the individuals He postpones till the Doomsday, but when it comes to the behavior of entire nations and communities, the rewards for good deeds and the punishments for bad ones are often delivered to them right here in this world. This point is explained in the following paragraphs.

Our Creator and Sustainer has provided the means to satisfy all human needs and urges, including the human desire for guidance. Almighty Allah (swt) established the institution of prophethood in order t guide humanity towards the Right Ideal. This is because the need to know the highest ideal of Beauty and Perfection, and the urge to love and worship that ideal, is the most irresistible desire of the human soul. A prophet or *nabi* is a person who is endowed with the knowledge, through Divine revelation or *Wahee*, that the only true Ideal worthy of our love and worship is none other than Almighty Allah (swt) Himself. The system of life based on this Ideal is characterized by an unconditional surrender to the will of the Creator, and this is what every prophet has preached to his people.

According to some traditions, there have been 124 thousand prophets in all, 313 of which were also messengers. Although the Qur'an does not clarify in an explicit manner the distinction between a prophet and a messenger, and hence there are a number of opinions on this point, the most logical explanation in our opinion is as follows. We believe that a prophet, or *nabi*, who was specifically appointed by Almighty Allah (swt) to guide a particular nation or community, got promoted to the rank of His envoy, in a manner of speaking, and therefore he would become a messenger, or *rasool*. This means that all messengers were chosen by Almighty Allah (swt) from among the prophets; that all messengers were prophets, but not all prophets were messengers.

The Holy Qur'an tells us that after the advent of a messenger or *rasool* to a given nation, the rise and fall of that nation became linked solely to its collective response to the Divine messenger. If the people surrendered to the commands of their Creator and obeyed His messenger, they enjoyed peace and prosperity and material comforts. But if they showed ingratitude, and refused to follow the Divine message, then they became liable for the most severe punishment from Almighty Allah (swt).

A community or a group of people who thus rejected the Divine messenger sent towards them became, in the sight of Allah (swt), an impediment to the overall evolution of humanity towards the ultimate realization of the Right Ideal. Therefore, the Divine plan for the human race demanded that such a useless and spiritually barren people be removed from the face of the earth, once and for all. This can be described as the law of "annihilation of the worst."

In this context, nearly identical stories of six different nations appear in the Qur'an, each of which was guilty of rejecting their Divinely appointed messengers. All of these nations were destroyed and eliminated as a punishment for their sins and transgressions. These condemned nations included, in chronological sequence, the people of Prophet Nuh (as), a nation called Aad to which Prophet Hud (as) was sent, a nation known as Thamud to which Prophet Saleh (as) was appointed, the twin cities of Sodom and Gomorrah which were assigned to Prophet Lut (as), the people of Prophet Sho'aib (as), and finally the Egyptian Pharaoh and his followers who rejected Prophet Musa (as). Of course, there may be numerous other nations who met this fate; although only six of these are mentioned in the

Holy Qur'an.

It should be kept in mind that such clear and open manifestations of the wrath of Almighty Allah (swt) used to appear in the past only after one of His messengers had explicitly and unambiguously communicated the Divine message to a particular group of people, and they remained persistent in refusing to surrender before the will of their Lord. The Qur'an is very emphatic on this point:

We never punish till We have sent a messenger. [TMQ Al-Isra 17:15]

But your Lord does not destroy habitations without having sent a messenger to their metropolis to read out Our commandments to them.

[TMQ Al-Qasas 28:59]

The converse of the above mentioned Divine Law is also true: A nation that unconditionally accepts the Sovereignty of Almighty Allah (swt), and acts accordingly, is blessed with all that is good and desirable in this world. This has been described by the Qur'an in several ways. Here are two examples:

And if they had followed the teachings of the Torah and the Gospel, and what has been sent down to them by their Lord, they would surely have enjoyed (blessings) from the heavens above and the earth below their feet. Some among them are moderate, but evil is what most of them do. [TMQ Al-Ma'ida 5:66]

But if the people of these regions had believed and feared God, We would surely have showered on them blessings of the heavens and the earth; but they only denied, and We punished them for their deeds.

[TMQ Al-A'raf 7:96]

The Qur'an maintains that the real and everlasting rewards for believing in and obeying the commands of Allah (swt) will manifest themselves in the next world, the Hereafter, or *Al-Aakhira*. However, there is a great deal to gain in this life as well, in the form of social harmony, peace, and general prosperity.

For those who do good there is good in the world, but certainly the abode of the next is better. [TMQ Al-Nahl 16:30]

Privileges & Obligations

A community that obeys the commands of Almighty Allah (swt) becomes dear to Him. This privilege is, however, coupled with many obligations. The more glories and bounties a nation is blessed with, the more are its responsibilities in the sight of Almighty Allah (swt). Privileges and obligations go together.

A community that claims to be the follower of a messenger of Allah (saw), and custodian of His message in the form of a revealed Book, automatically becomes the representative of the Almighty among other nations. This is a tremendous responsibility. If the behavior of such a community is in contravention to its claim, then, according to Divine Justice, they deserve all the humiliation and disgrace, sufferings and miseries in the life of this world. If their character and morals, their way of life, their society and culture, and their politico-economic norms are contrary to the teachings of the Divine Revelation, then this constitutes an unpardonable crime. The reason is that such behavior, instead of presenting an attractive and true picture of the way of life based on the Right Ideal — and thereby bringing people nearer to Allah (swt) — serves only to repel them away from the Divine Guidance by displaying a distorted and ugly image of that guidance. The Qur'an is very explicit on this point:

O you who believe, why do you profess what you do not practice? Saying what you do not practice is most hateful in the sight of God. [TMQ Al-Saff 61:2,3]

Do you believe a part of the Book and reject a part? There is no other award for them who so act but ignominy in this world, and on the Day of Judgment the severest of punishment. [TMQ Al-Baqarah 2:85]

A strange characteristic of such disgraced communities is that, in spite of receiving frequent installments of Divine punishment, they continue to believe that Allah (swt) truly loves them. Due to this self-deception, which is based upon their claimed association with a holy messenger of Allah (swt), they continue to live in a fool's paradise of their own making. They feel satisfied in the unfounded conviction that they deserve, as a birthright, some kind of preferential treatment from their Lord, just because they belong to a particular community and for no other reason. The Qur'an tries to shake such complacent people from their deluded slumber thus:

The Jews and the Christians say: "We are sons of God and beloved of Him." Say: "Why does He punish you then for your sins? No! You are only mortals, of His creation." [TMQ Al-Ma'ida 5:18]

And they (the Jews) say: "Hell fire will not touch us for more than a few days." Say: "Have you so received a promise from God? Then surely God will not withdraw His pledge. Or do you impute things to God of which you have no knowledge at all?" [TMQ Al-Baqarah 2:80]

Unfortunately, the image we get from these verses is a disturbingly true representation of today's Muslims. Even the repeated episodes of severe punishments, in the background of continuous sufferings, has failed to produce in us any sense of guilt or remorse. Instead, our deeply ingrained myth of being a privileged people has remained intact. Unbelievable as it may sound, the more disgrace we receive, the more we fall in love with ourselves, blinded by our supposed righteousness and delusion of our own grandeur. Such irony, however, may well be a part of our punishment.

The Present and former Muslim Ummah

The word "Islam" stands for submission before the Sovereignty of Almighty Allah (swt), as proclaimed by His prophets throughout human history. The number of these holy men, as mentioned earlier, is reported to be 124 thousand. However, irrespective of the exact figure, it is generally accepted by scholars of the Qur'an that five of them are the most prominent and most notable. These include Prophet Nuh (as), Prophet Ibrahim (as), Prophet Musa (as), Prophet Isa (as), and Prophet Muhammad (saw).

Out of these, Prophet Nuh (as) was probably not endowed with any Divine Scripture. Prophet Ibrahim (as) did receive some sort of scriptures, but there was no formal law or *Shari'ah* in them. Similarly, the *Zabur* or Psalms of Prophet Dawood (as) and the *Injeel* or Gospel of Prophet Isa (as) contained nothing that can be described as law; instead, they were composed of hymns and exhortations, respectively. It follows that, among the known Divine Revelations, only two can be described as "Books," in the sense that they contained *Shari'ah,* — the Torah (or *Tauraat*) and the Holy Qur'an. The former is the name given to the "Five Books of Moses," also called the *Pentateuch*, which are included in the beginning of the Old Testament. The latter, i.e., the Holy Qur'an, is the final and ultimate Book as revealed to Prophet Muhammad (saw).

It is significant to note that the Torah was revealed to Prophet Musa (as) as a guidance only for the Israelites, whereas the Qur'an — being the last of Revelations — describes itself as "The Guidance" for the whole humanity, for all times to come.

The main conclusion of the above discussion, however, is that there had been only two Muslim "*Ummahs*" during the entire period of known human history. This is because the genesis of such a community is always preceded by — and is the direct result of — a *Shari'ah* being given to a messenger and through him to his followers. Since there had been only two versions of the Divine Law that we can be sure about, i.e., the Mosaic Law and the *Shari'ah* of Prophet Muhammad (saw), it follows that there had been only two Muslim *Ummahs* — the Israelites or the Jews who were the previous *Ummah*, and the community of the followers of Prophet Muhammad (saw), which constitutes the current and final *Ummah*.

Next, we shall discuss the common features and distinguishing characteristics of these two communities, along with a brief review of their history and the present state of their affairs. The relevance of this topic is based upon the fact that, according to the predictions of Prophet Muhammad (saw), the Muslims and the Jews of the world — as custodians of Divine Revelations — are going to act as two key players with regard to the ultimate destiny of mankind.

Certain pointers of the Qur'an and detailed prophecies in the *Hadith* literature predict the events that would happen before the end of the world, that is, they foretell the final acts of the global drama. It is vital to comprehend these predictions with reference to their proper background, not only to clear our minds of any distrust or doubt, but also to prevent any feeling of bewilderment when that which has been promised does take place.

Another reason for discussing the history of the previous *Ummah*, as will be elucidated shortly, is the stunning resemblance between the history of Jews and that of Muslims, a fact that was also foretold by Prophet Muhammad (saw).

Common Denominators

The Jews remained the sole custodians of the Divine Message and His Book for almost two millennia — from about 1350 B.C., when Prophet Musa (AS) was given Torah and the Covenant with the Israelites took place at Sinai, to 624 C.E., when the change of *qibla* from Jerusalem to Makkah symbolically announced the birth of a new *Ummah.*

The Jews were relegated from their rank because of their transgressions and haughtiness. The Qur'an severely criticizes and upbraids them for their long record of ingratitude and repeated violations of Divine injunctions, and declares them a condemned people. These reprimands were issued by Almighty Allah (swt) because of the continued failure, on the part of the Jews, to carry out their responsibilities as custodians of the Divine Revelation. From the Second year of *Hijrah* onwards, the followers of Prophet Muhammad (saw) were appointed as guardians of the Message of God, as well as His representatives among all nations. Thus, this supreme blessing of Almighty Allah (swt), i.e., His revealed guidance in the form of a Book, is something common to both the Jews and the Muslims, although the Hebrew scriptures are no longer in their pure and unadulterated state. In this context the following verse appears twice in the Qur'an:

Remember, O Children of Israel, the favors I bestowed on you and made you most exalted among the nations of the world.

[TMQ Al-Baqarah 2:47 & 122]

Another point of convergence between the Jews and the Muslims is the prominent personality of Prophet Ibrahim (AS), the patriarch who is equally revered by the followers of both faiths. The Jews, of course, are the descendants of Prophet Ishaq (AS), younger son of Prophet Ibrahim (AS). Similarly, the earliest Muslims were Arabs — the descendants of Prophet Ibrahim's elder son Prophet Isma'el (AS) — and they constitute today the nucleus of the Muslim *Ummah*. But irrespective of this genealogical relationship, the whole of the Muslim *Ummah* has an attitude of veneration and high regard for Prophet Ibrahim (AS), as they consider him to be their spiritual father.

The difference between Us & Them

There are two important features which not only distinguish the Muslims from the Jews but also prove the former's clear superiority over the latter. The first is related to the fact that the present Muslim *Ummah* is collectively responsible to preach and spread the Message of Almighty Allah (swt), and to try her utmost for establishing the domination of Islam over the entire globe. This stupendous duty is, in fact, a logical corollary of the culmination of Prophethood.

The most outstanding characteristic of the advent of Prophet Muhammad (saw) is that the institution of prophethood has reached its acme of perfection with his advent. Since the ultimate echelon of prophetic evolution has been reached, it follows that there shall be no more prophets. But the world has not yet ended, and the humanity is still thirsty for the knowledge of the Real and still yearning for a just social system. This can only mean one thing: The Muslim *Ummah* is now responsible, as a whole, to continue the work of the prophets.

The Qur'an proclaims that the purpose behind the advent of Prophet Muhammad (saw) is the establishment of the ascendancy and domination of Islam over all aspects of life, all over the world. The following words appear thrice in the Holy Qur'an, defining the manifesto for a global Islamic Revolution:

It is He who sent His Messenger with The Guidance (Al-Qur'an) and the true way of life (Deen-al- Haq), in order to make it prevail over the entire mode of living. [TMQ Al-Taubah 9:33; Al-Fath 48:28; & Al- Saff 61:9]

Unlike previous messengers of God, the advent of Prophet Muhammad (saw) was not just for his own nation, the people of Arabia, but it was also directed towards all mankind in general, for all times to come. Again, unlike the Jews, who were asked only to act in accordance with the Mosaic law, the Muslims have a much extensive and arduous responsibility on their shoulders, that is, they are obliged to guide and lead the entire humanity. Muslims are required to obey the commands of God in their own lives, to preach God's Message worldwide and in every generation till the end of the world, and to struggle tirelessly with the objective of making Islam dominant as a socio-political order. The previous Muslim *Ummah*, in contrast, was never required to perform all these duties.

The second point of difference between the Jews and the Muslims is that, in contrast to the former who were a uniracial community (being composed of only the "Children of Israel," i.e., the descendants of Prophet Yaqoob), the present Muslim *Ummah* is a multiracial and multinational community. The Jews themselves, or any other nation for that matter, can join the Muslim *Ummah* anytime they want — by accepting Prophet Muhammad (saw) as the final Messenger of God; their race, color, language, or previous creed notwithstanding.

The Muslim *Ummah* is basically a diverse group of people belonging to all kinds of different national, ethnic, and linguistic backgrounds. In general, however, the Muslim *Ummah* can be seen as being composed of two distinct components: the descendants of Prophet Isma'el (AS), referred to in the Qur'an as *ummiyean* (the unlettered people), as well as all other peoples and nations, referred to in the Qur'an as *aakhereen* (those of later time).

In other words, the Muslim *Ummah* is made up of a nucleus or a core of Arabs, surrounded by non- Arab nations, whether they be Kurds or Turks, Persians or Indian, Afghans or Muhgals, Black of African origin or Whites of European descent. The common element or the binding force that brings all of them together and keeps them united — at least in theory — is obviously their faith and ideology, that is, Islam.

It is rather gratifying to learn that we Muslims enjoy a two-fold superiority over the Jews. But it doesn't take a genius to realize that being superior also means that we have to fulfill many more responsibilities and obligations. The Jews were repeatedly punished for their collective crimes, but if we were to follow in their footsteps then this would make us liable to a chastisement much more severe than what they received.

Similarly, the most prominent part of the Muslim *Ummah* — the Arabs — also enjoy a form of superiority vis-à-vis other Muslims; this is because Prophet Muhammad (saw) was one of them, and because God's final Message was revealed in their own language. But, as we have described above, the fact is that the more privileged you are, the greater is your responsibility. The Arab Muslims have, in general, failed to live up to their exceptionally privileged position as the primary custodians of Divine Message, thereby making themselves liable to Divine retribution. It follows that the main impact of any major episode of Divine punishment, that might befall the Muslims, will have to be endured by the Arabs. This was foretold by Prophet Muhammad (saw), as we shall see later on.

A backward Glance

We now turn to the history of Jews, in the hope that the Muslims might learn something from their ups and down.

By the time when the Qur'an was being revealed to Prophet Muhammad (saw), the Jews had already passed through two phases of rise and two phases of decline. In general, they enjoyed material prosperity and political domination as long as they acted righteously, and suffered from misery and slavery and persecution whenever they rebelled against the Divine commands. The Jews were invited, through the Qur'an — and that invitation is still open — to accept Prophet Muhammad (saw) as the last Messenger of God and to repent for their collective sins. They were clearly warned that rejecting Prophet Muhammad (saw) and the Qur'an would mean that their humiliation will continue. The Qur'an proclaims:

We announced to the Children of Israel in the Book: "You will surely create disorder twice in the land, and become exceedingly arrogant." So, when the time of the first prediction came, We sent against you Our creatures full of martial might, who ransacked your cities; and the prediction was fulfilled. Then We gave you a chance against them, and strengthened you with wealth and children, and increased your numbers (and said): "If you do good, you will do so for your own good; if you do evil, you will do it for your own loss." So when the time of the second prediction came, (We roused against you another people) to ravage you, and to enter the Temple as they had done the first time, and to destroy utterly what they conquered. Your Lord may haply be merciful to you. But if you repeat (the crime), We shall repeat (the punishment).

[TMQ Al-Isra 17:4-9]

In order to comprehend these historical events, alluded to in the above verses, and to appreciate their significance with regard to the Muslims of the world, we must go back in time.

As mentioned before, Jews are the descendants of Prophet Yaqoob (as) — also known as Israel — son of Prophet Ishaq (AS), son of Prophet Ibrahim (as). Prophet Ibrahim (as) had migrated, nearly 4000 years ago, from the city of Ur in the Euphrates Valley (now Iraq) to Cannan (now divided between Jordan and Israel), along with his wife Prophet Sarah (as) and nephew Prophet Lut (as). Prophet Ibrahim (as) acquired a second wife, Hajrah (SA), who bore him Isma'el, when he was 86 years old. Then, at the ripe old age of 100, Sarah (SA) gave birth to his second son, Ishaq. Prophet Ibrahim (AS) established two centers for the spread of God's word, one in Makkah where he settled Hajirah (SA) and her son Prophet Isma'el (AS), and the other in Palestine where he settled Sarah (SA) and her son Prophet Ishaq (AS). This gave rise to the birth of two great nations, *Banu Isma'el* and *Banu Israel,* as promised by Almighty Allah (swt). According to the Old Testament:

God said to Abraham: "Look up at the sky, and count the stars, if you can. So many will your descendants be." (Genesis 15:5)

Early Jewish History

Prophet Yousuf (AS) — the grandson of Prophet Ishaq (AS) — was able to rise to the top in the kingdom of Egypt, after being sold there as a slave because of a malevolent sibling rivalry. Prophet Yousuf (AS) then invited his father and his eleven brothers and their families — 70 strong — to Egypt, and helped them settle in a hospitable and congenial country. This most probably happened during the period of the Hyksos dynasty.

The Israelites continued to grow during the next 400 year, and developed their famous twelve tribes. Initially they enjoyed a life of prosperity and were respected by the locals. However, after the decline of the Semitic Shepherd kings in about 1550 B.C., they were increasingly seen as aliens, and therefore a security risk, by the nationalist Pharaohs of the nineteenth dynasty. As a result, the rulers started to abuse and exploit them as slaves, and even adopted a policy of ethnic cleansing towards them.

Their miseries continued until Almighty Allah (swt) raised Prophet Musa (AS) as His messenger. He rose as a charismatic leader of the Israelites, and, after a long struggle with the Pharaoh, freed them from bondage. The migration of the Israelites from Egypt, called the "Exodus," most probably took place around 1350 B.C.. The Holy Qur'an reminds the Jews of Allah's benevolence thus:

Remember, We saved you from the Pharaoh's people who wronged and oppressed you and slew your sons but spared your women. In this was a great trial from your Lord. Remember, We parted the sea and saved you, and drowned the men of Pharaoh before your very eyes.

[TMQ Al-Baqarah 2:49,50]

Prophet Musa (AS) led the Israelites into the Sinai peninsula, at the Northern tip of which lays Mount Sinai — or *Jebel Musa* — the present day site of St. Catherine's Monastery. It was here that Almighty Allah (swt) gave him the guidance for his people in the form of Torah. The famous Covenant with Israelites also took place, when they promised to obey Allah's commands and, in return, they were promised constant care, prosperity, and victory over their enemies.

Prophet Musa (AS) and his people then went about a hundred and fifty miles north of Mount Sinai, into the wilderness of Paran, at the Southern border of what was then called Cannan. According to the Old Testament, Almighty Allah (swt) said to Prophet Musa (AS):

"Send men out to explore Canaan, the land which I am going to give to the Israelites." (Numbers 13:2)

Twelve spies were sent, one from each tribe, and they returned after forty days to report that the Promised land was flowing with milk and honey. However, except for two of them — Joshua and Caleb — they weren't willing to go to war, saying that the towns were fortified, their inhabitants formidable and of gigantic stature. Hearing such discouraging reports, the Israelites simply refused to fight, despite all attempts to persuade and convince them. The Bible vividly portrays the scene of their refusal:

The whole Israelite community cried out in dismay and the people wept all night long. Everyone complained against Moses and Aaron: "If only we had died in Egypt or in the wilderness!" they said, "why should the Lord bring us to this land, to die in battle and leave our wives and our dependents to become the spoils of war? It would be better for us to go back to Egypt." And they spoke of choosing someone to lead them back there. (Numbers

14:1-4)

As a result of their cowardliness and lack of faith, the Promised Land was withheld from the Israelites for a period of forty years. Almighty Allah (swt) condemned the Israelites to wander in the wilderness of Sinai for a full generation. The Holy Qur'an narrates this whole incidence as follows:

(Musa said) "Enter, O my people, the Holy Land that God has ordained for you, and do not turn back, or you will suffer." They said: "O Musa, in that land live a people who are formidable; we shall never go there until they leave. We shall enter when they go away." Then two of the men who feared (God), and to whom God was gracious [i.e., Joshua and Caleb] said to them: "Charge and rush the gate. If you enter, you will surely be victorious. And place your trust in God if you truly believe." They said: "O Musa, we shall never, never enter as long as they are there. Go you and your Lord to fight them; we stay here." (Musa) said, "O Lord, I have control over none but myself and my brother; so draw a dividing line between us and these, the wicked people." (And God) said: "Then verily this Land is forbidden them for forty years, and they shall wander perplexed over the earth. So do not grieve for these, the wicked people."

[TMQ Al-Ma'ida 5:21-26]

Israel's Golden Age

The men who had set out from Egypt under Prophet Musa (AS) were utterly devoid of any sense of honor or self-respect, and they lacked the necessary courage and fortitude to face their enemies in battle. The reason for their low morale was obviously their centuries long slavery and persecution in Egypt. During their forty years wandering, however, the older generation perished and was replaced by a new generation that grew up in an environment of total freedom. As a result, this fresh generation had a strong enough character to invade the Holy Land under the leadership of Joshua, the successor of Prophet Musa (AS). The Israelites were thus able to conquer most of the cities, despite the fact that their enemies had fortified towns, advanced weapons, and swift chariots.

The conquest of the Promised Land, however, remained incomplete. Instead of destroying the numerous nations inhabiting Palestine, as they were told to do, the Israelites fell victim to tribal parochialism. They failed to establish a single unified kingdom of their own, and divided the Land among themselves. Thus, losing their political and military strength, the Israelites were forced to live side by side with the corrupt and idolatrous communities of their time. This not only resulted very soon in their adopting all the moral evils of Amorites, Jebusites, and Canaanites, etc., but also in their being driven out from a major part of Palestine by the incessant attacks of the unconquered nations, especially the Philistines.

At last the Israelites felt the need to preserve their independence and regain their unity. A delegation of elders from each tribe gathered and requested their prophet — Samuel — to appoint for them a ruler, who chose

Saul (or *Taloot*) as the king of Israelites. This episode of Jewish history is also mentioned in the Holy Qur'an (Al-Baqarah 2:243-248), and took place around 1020 B.C.. Taloot was later succeeded by Prophet Dawood (AS) and Prophet Suleman (AS), and under the rule of these three great kings, the Israelites were able to transform themselves from a small group of quarreling tribes into the most powerful kingdom between the Nile and Euphrates. During the years 1020 B.C. and 922 B.C., Israel reached the zenith of its territorial size and political power, enjoying an era of peace and affluence. Culture, trade, and industry flourished, especially during the reign of Prophet Suleman (AS). The famous Temple was also built for the first time in Jerusalem.

First Period of Decline

The death of Prophet Suleman (AS) — or King Solomon, as he is called in the Bible — marks the beginning of the first period of decline for the Israelites. The united monarchy disappeared, and in its place arose two kingdoms — Israel in the north and Judah in the south. The people of the northern kingdom crowned Jeroboam, an official who had rebelled against King Solomon and taken refuge in Egypt, and he made Shechem his royal city. The southern kingdom continued to be ruled by the Davidic dynasty, its first monarch being Rehoboam, son of Solomon, with its center at Jerusalem.

Although both kingdoms were strife-ridden from the very beginning, Israel was especially turbulent because of its large population which seldom agreed on anything. Politically unstable, the northern kingdom suffered a prolonged period of internal warfare until 876 B.C., when an army officer Omri got hold of the throne and built a new capital at Samaria. He, however, adopted a policy of compromise with paganism, as a result of which the common people began to assimilate various polytheistic practices of the neighboring communities. The rise of paganism became especially serious under Omri's son Ahab, who married a Phoenician princess, Jezebel. She started a ruthless campaign to wipe out Israel's traditional monotheism, and to replace it with the Canaanite fertility cult and the worship of Baal. Two prophets, Prophet Elias (AS) or Elijah and Prophet Al-Yasa (AS) or Elisha, rose and tried their best to warn their people, and to check their growing inclination towards paganism, but the cult of Baal and the associated rituals of licentious dances remained irresistibly attractive for the austere Israelites.

At last, Almighty Allah's anger manifested itself in the form of Assyrians from the north, whose takeover of Israel started gradually but ended with severe subjugation. Initially, the kings of Israel were forced to pay tribute money to Assyria, but in 721 B.C., the Assyrian armies, under king Sargon, attacked and plundered Samaria, killing thousands of her inhabitants. According to an Assyrian inscription, King Sargon carried away 27,290 Israelites into captivity, and scattered them in his eastern provinces, terminating the existence of the northern kingdom as an independent nation.

On the other hand, the history of the southern state of Judah displays a relatively slower degeneration in beliefs and morality. However, they too started to indulge in idol-worship and transgressions of the Divine Law, becoming more and more corrupt with every passing generation. Prophet Isaiah rose and tried to reform his people during the period 740 B.C. to 700 B.C.. His warnings and prophecies — which were collected in the "Book of Isaiah" of the Old Testament — clearly testify to the moral decadence of his times. Here are a few statements from his sermons:

You sinful nation, a people weighed down with iniquity, a race of evildoers, children whose lives are depraved, who have deserted the Lord, spurned the Holy One of Israel, and turned your backs on him! Why do you invite more punishment, why persist in your defection? Your head is all covered with sores, your whole body is bruised;

(Isaiah 1:4,5)

Your rulers are rebels, associates of thieves; every one of them loves a bribe and chases after gifts; they deny the fatherless their rights and the widow's cause is never heard. (Isaiah 1:23)

Once again the Lord spoke to me; he said: Because this nation has rejected the waters of Shiloah, which flow softly and gently, therefore the Lord will bring up against it the mighty flood waters of the Euphrates. The river will rise in its channels and overflow all its banks.

In a raging torrent mounting neck-high it will sweep through Judah. With his outspread wings the whole expanse of the land will be filled, for God is with us.

Take note, you nations; you will be shattered. Listen, all you distant parts of the earth: arm yourselves, and be shattered; arm yourselves, and be shattered. Devise your plans, but they will be foiled; propose what you will, but it will not be carried out; for God is with us. (Isaiah 8:5-10)

Then came Prophet Jeremiah, who tried to shake his people out of their perverted ways, idolatry, and apostasy, during the period 627 B.C. to 587 B.C.. His sermons, however, met with an intense opposition from a corrupt society that was addicted to idol-worship to the point of fanaticism. His teachings were later collected as the "Book of Jeremiah" in the Old Testament, from which the following excerpts are taken:

Listen to the words of the Lord, people of Jacob, all you families of Israel. These are the words of the Lord:

What fault did your forefathers find in me, that they went so far astray from me, pursuing worthless idols
and becoming worthless like them;
that they did not ask, "Where is the Lord, who brought us up from Egypt
and led us through the wilderness, through a barren and broken country, a country parched and forbidding,
where no one ever traveled, where no one made his home?
I brought you into a fertile land to enjoy its fruit and every good thing in it,
but when you entered my land you defiled it and made loathsome the home I gave you.
The priests no longer asked, 'Where is the Lord?'
Those who handled the law had no real knowledge of me, the shepherds of the people rebelled against me;
the prophets prophesied in the name of Baal and followed gods who were powerless to help.

(Jeremiah 2:4-8)

Stop before your feet are bare and your throat is parched. But you said, 'No, I am desperate.
I love foreign gods and I must go after them.

As a thief is ashamed when he is found out so the people of Israel feel ashamed,
they, their kings, their princes, their priests, and their prophets, who say to a block of wood, 'You are our father'
and cry 'Mother' to a stone.
On me they have turned their backs and averted their faces from me. Yet in

their time of trouble theysay, 'Rise up and save us!'
Where are the gods you made for yourselves?
In your time of trouble let them arise and save you. For you, Judah, have as many gods as you have towns. (Jeremiah 2:25-28)

Israel, I am bringing against you a distant nation,
an ancient people established long ago, says the Lord, a people whose language you do not know,
whose speech you will not understand; they are all mighty warriors,
their jaws are a grave, wide open,
to devour your harvest and your food, to devour your sons and your daughters, to devour your flocks and your herds,
to devour your vines and your fig trees They will beat down with the sword the walled cities in which you trust. (Jeremiah 5:15-17)

Despite all these explicit and unambiguous warnings — delivered to the inhabitants of Judah by two of their great prophets — there was no sign of any remorse or repentance whatsoever. Instead, the Israelites stubbornly continued in their pagan practices and disobedience of Divine injunction, thereby inviting the wrath of Almighty Allah (swt).

Divine punishment first appeared in the form of Babylonian forces marching into Judah in 604 B.C., when King Jehoiakim acquiesced without any struggle and agreed to pay heavy tribute to Nebuchadnezzar, the king of Babylonia. He, however, rebelled against his Babylonian overlords in 601 B.C., resulting in the first siege of Jerusalem that lasted three months. The armies of Nebuchadnezzar entered the Holy City on March 15, 597 B.C., and plundered the Temple of Solomon. They decimated the society by deporting the new King Jehoiachin (Jehoiakim's son), his family, noblemen, and thousands of influential citizens, soldiers, and skilled craftsmen as captives to Babylonia. Nebuchadnezzar then placed the king's uncle Zedekiah on the throne of Judah. Soon Zedekiah also became involved in a conspiracy against Babylonia, resulting in the second siege of Jerusalem. This time the city remained under siege for 18 months, and the conditions deteriorated to such an extent that some of the inhabitants were forced to eat human flesh.

Finally, the wall of Jerusalem was breached on July 9, 587 B.C.. The rebellious vassal king was captured and was forced to watch as his sons were slaughtered. Then he was blinded and taken in chains to Babylonia, where he later died in prison.

Nebuchadnezzar decided to make an example of the city, and his orders were carried out with cruel thoroughness. The city walls were demolished. The Temple and the palace were stripped of all valuables and burned to the ground. Thousands were killed, and a large part of the population was taken as captives to Babylonia, more than 500 miles away. The kingdom of Judah itself became a Babylonian province, which presented at that time a deeply scarred look. Everywhere, towns were ransacked and burned, crops destroyed, and villages deserted.

Reform & Revival the Maccabees

The destruction of the northern kingdom of Israel by the Assyrians was irreversibly complete and final. The dispersed Jews lost their distinct identity as they merged with and vanished among the neighboring nations, especially the conquerors. In contrast, the Babylonian exile was only a harsh reminder from Almighty Allah (swt) to the inhabitants of Judah.

Although the exiles were not subjected to blatant slavery, the impact of captivity was still soul- crushing for them. They must have felt humiliated and anguished with the memory of their abject defeat and ongoing bondage, as depicted in the poetry composed during that period (see "*Lamentations*"' in the Old Testament). In Babylonia, the Jews were made targets of contempt and derision; they were required to toil hard and pay tribute money in exchange for their existence. Those of noble origin were particularly treated with indignity, adding the pain of insult to their already injured souls.

All this must have melted their hearts and caused them to repent. There were a number of active reformers, both among the captives and among those who remained in Judah, preaching and exhorting everyone to fulfill their part of the Covenant. Most prominent among these voices of reform was that of Prophet Ezekiel, who had been brought to Babylonia during the first deportation in 597 B.C.. He called his people towards God, inspiring them to mend their ways and atone for their sins. He announced that God is going to give the Israelites another chance to repent, and that He will cause them to return to Jerusalem. The following statements are taken from the "Book of Ezekiel" in the Old Testament:

This word of the Lord came to me:
O man, when the Israelites were living on their own soil they defiled it with their ways and deeds; their ways were loathsome and unclean in my sight. I poured out my fury on them for the blood they had poured out on the land, and for the idols with which they had defiled it. I scattered them among the nations, and they were dispersed in many lands. I passed a sentence on them which their ways and deeds deserved.

(Ezekiel 36:16-19)

It is not for the sake of you Israelites that I am acting, but for the sake of my holy name...I shall take you from among the nations and gather you from every land, and bring you to your homeland. I shall sprinkle pure water over you, and you will be purified from everything that defiles you; I shall purify you from the taint of all your idols. I shall give you a new heart and put a new spirit within you; I shall remove the heart of stone from your body and give you a heart of flesh. I shall put my spirit within you and make you conform to my statutes; you will observe my laws faithfully. Then you will live in the land I gave to your forefathers; you will be my people, and I shall be your God.

(Ezekiel 36:22,24-28)

God's mercy came in the shape of Cyrus, king of Persia, who, after conquering Media and Lydia, brought the Babylonian Empire to her knees in 539 B.C., thus laying down the foundations of the Great Persian Empire. The very next year, Cyrus authorized the Jews in Mesopotamia to return to Jerusalem and rebuild their Temple at the expense of the royal treasury. He then appointed Sheshbazzar, probably the son of King Jehoiachin, to rule Judah as a semi-independent state. Sheshbazzar led the first group of Jews back to their homeland, followed by another expedition led by Zerubbabel in 522 B.C.. However, because of a number of reasons, the rebuilding of the Temple could not progress beyond the laying down of its foundations. Eighteen years latter, Zerubbabel became Judah's governor who, supported by Prophets Haggai and Zechariah and the high-priest Jeshua, completed the second Temple in 515 B.C..

In 443 B.C., Persian king Artaxerxes I allowed Zehemiah, one of his Jew attendants, to supervise the building of the walls of Jerusalem, and later appointed him governor of Judah as a separate province. Prophet Uzair (AS) — otherwise known as Ezra — arrived in Jerusalem in 398 B.C., with the mission of re- establishing religious purity and obedience to the Mosaic Law. He persuaded all Jewish men to divorce their pagan wives and proscribed mixed marriages in the future. He also demanded strict adherence to Sabbath and the dietary laws. He took a pledge from his people that they would worship none other that God. A major achievement of Prophet Uzair (AS) was that he re-compiled the five Books of Moses, or the Torah, which were lost during the destruction of Jerusalem.

The process of Jewish revival suffered a set back with the rise of Greeks, and the defeat of the Persians by Alexander in 333 B.C.. After the death of Alexander, his kingdom was divided among his generals. Egypt came under the control of Ptolemy, whose descendants ruled Judah for the next hundred years. Seleucus had established his own dynasty over Babylonia and Syria, whereas Palestine was incorporated into this kingdom by Antiochus III in 198 B.C..

Earlier, Alexander had initiated a policy of implanting the Greek culture — Hellenism — in his conquered lands. As a result, during all these years of Greek rule, the Jews became divided into two groups. Those living in Egypt and other places outside Judah, called "Jews of the Dispersion," started adopting Greek ideas, dress, language, and life-style. The sacred scriptures had to be translated in Greek as most of them could no longer comprehend their original language, Hebrew. Mixed marriages became common once again, and circumcision was increasingly ignored. A popular Hellensitic idea — that different nations simply worshipped the same God with different names — became acceptable among these "progressive" Jews. On the other hand, there were those orthodox ones — or "fundamentalists" in contemporary terminology — who persisted with the traditional Jewish beliefs and culture, as the spirit of revival infused by Prophet Uzair (AS) was still very active among them.

In 175 B.C., Antiochus IV came to the throne, and used Hellenization to wipe out both monotheism and the Mosaic Law. He promoted Greek customs and ideas with the help of his aristocratic Jewish collaborators. Pagan altars were set up, religious celebrations and services forbidden, circumcision outlawed, and possession of Torah declared a capital crime. This only sharpened the distinction between the progressive and orthodox Jews, and motivated the latter ones to rebel.

An elderly priest named Mathathias rejected the attempts to cultivate and encourage such outrageous disobedience of the Divine commands. He, along with his five sons, started a revolt in the form of guerrilla warfare. Soon, a group of zealous Jews joined them, who were known as "Hasideans," or the pious ones. An army of devoted Israelites was formed which began a full-fledged revolutionary struggle against their Syrian oppressors, and this came to be called as the "Maccabee" uprising. A long series of battle followed, where these small, untrained, and ill-equipped group of men were able to defeat their much superior rivals. This ultimately led to the establishment of the "Great Maccabee Empire," marking the second phase of rise and domination for the Israelites.

The religious fervor and sincerity among the Jews, however, started to subside with the passage of time. The love of God began to be gradually replaced by the craving for material comforts and wealth. The spirit of morality disappeared, leaving behind the empty form of rituals. Internal conflicts led to a split among the Jews, so much so that some of them invited the Roman general Pompey to come to Palestine. But once the Roman army had arrived, it would not leave.

The second Era of Decline

In 63 B.C Pompey, after taking over the old Sleucid Empire of Syria, turned towards Jerusalem. Thousands of Jews were killed during the three month long siege of the Holy City, and by the time the Roman army broke through the walls of Jerusalem, they were killing each other in confusion.

The Romans abolished the Maccabean dynasty and appointed Antipater as their puppet ruler. But soon after Julius Caesar's murder in 44 B.C, Antipater was poisoned and a civil war ensued in Palestine with different groups vying for dominance. To restore order, the Romans nominated a clever Jew named Herod as their viceroy to rule the Israelites. Herod reigned for the next 33 years by patronizing the Jewish religious hierarchy on the one hand, and propagating the Greco-Roman culture and showing his faithfulness to Caesar on the other hand. In order to demonstrate his loyalty to Judaism, he ordered a reconstruction of the second Temple. The result was the largest and most magnificent building complex of the ancient world. At the same time, the moral degeneration of the Jews continued and reached its lowest ebb during the reign of Herod.

After Herod's death, his kingdom was divided among his three sons: (a) Archelaus became the ruler of Smaria, Judeae, and northern Edom, but was replaced in 6 C.E. by a Roman governor; (b) Antipas became the head of Galilee and Jordan in northern Palestine; whereas (c) Philip ruled the land between river Yermuk and Mt. Hermon

It is significant to note that during all those years of indirect Roman rule, the Jews had, in general, enjoyed full religious autonomy. The Romans would obviously intervene in matters of political or military nature, but the everyday administration of justice and local affairs — like the Sanhedrin court in Jerusalem

— were left wholly to the Jewish officials responsible for applying the Mosaic Law.

It was this Jewish court, Sanhedrin, that convicted God's last messenger to the Children of Israel — Jesus Christ or Prophet Isa (AS) — of blasphemy, and requested death sentence from the Roman governor Pontius Pilate. The collective rejection of Prophet Isa (AS) by the Israelites was not a minor crime in the sight of Almighty Allah (swt) — as he was Allah's *Rasool*, or envoy. This time Divine punishment appeared in the form of Roman armies, and the Holy City was destroyed for the second time.

The Romans had appointed Agrippa I, grandson of Herod the Great, to rule the territories that were once under Herod himself. Soon afterwards, a serious protest against the Romans led to an open Jewish revolt in 66 C.E., which neither King Agrippa II nor the Roman procurator was able to contain. The Romans retaliated with full military might, ultimately leading to the destruction of Jerusalem in 70 C.E. by the armies of General Titus. The loss of life among the Jews was incredibly high, as 133 thousand are reported to have been killed in Jerusalem alone. Thousands were made slaves, starved to death, or killed in Roman amphitheaters. Herod's Temple was burned and completely demolished.

Emperor Hadrian later built a new Roman colony, called Aelia Capitolina, over the desolate ruins of Jerusalem. However, the Jews were banished from their Holy City and were not allowed to re-enter for the next half a millennium.

As mentioned before, the advent of Prophet Muhammad (saw) in the 7th century C.E. constituted a golden opportunity for the Jews to escape from the wrath of God the Almighty. They, however, not only rejected the Prophethood of Muhammad (saw) as a community, but also earned the unenviable reputation of being the worst enemy of Islam and Muslims. As a result, their second era of decline has continued till the present, and they remained, to this date, a condemned and disgraced people. We shall return to this topic after a while.

Two of a kind

The rationale behind going through all these details of Jewish history is to be able to see our faces in their mirror. Both the Muslims and the Jews claim to be the followers of a holy messenger of Almighty Allah (swt), and both were endowed with Divine Scriptures. This in itself constitutes a significant common factor, meaning that the two are essentially similar communities. According to a tradition that appears in *Jame' Tirmidhi*, Prophet Muhammad (saw) is reported to have said: "My *Ummah* will undergo and experience all those conditions which were experienced by the Children of Israel, just as a shoe resembles its pair." The parallelism between the history of Muslims and that of Jews is indeed amazing. A comparative study of their past reveals that, like the Israelites, we Muslims have also undergone two phases of rise and two phases of decline, as alluded to by Prophet Muhammad (saw) in the above prediction.

What follows, therefore, is an outline of the history of Muslims vis-à-vis their rise and decline over the last fourteen centuries, and this will clearly demonstrate the points of resemblance between the Jews and Muslims.

The principal reason, however, for presenting this comprehensive yet brief chronological sketch of our past is two fold: First, as far as "rise" is concerned, we need to fully appreciate our past grandeur and glories, so that our younger generations can be motivated to recapture that lost greatness and to try and revive this half-dead tiger that was once the Muslim *Ummah*. Second, with reference to "decline," we need to clearly understand that Allah's Justice is the same for everyone, and His laws are permanent and immutable. The manner in which He treated the previous Muslim *Ummah* — the Jews — was repeated in His dealings with us. When we indulged in the same sins and crimes as were committed by the Jews, we received the same punishment as was given to them.

To begin with, we need to have in our minds a rough idea of the geography of Muslim world. For the purpose of description, the Muslim world can be seen as consisting of three sections. That is, the *center* or the heart of Muslim world, which is made up of the Arabian peninsula in the south and Iraq, Palestine, Syria, and Asia Minor in the north; the *right wing*, which extends from Iran, Afghanistan, Pakistan, and Central Asian republics to Malaysia and Indonesia in the Far East; and finally the *left wing*, which includes the whole North Africa and, in the good old days, extended even upto Spain.

The Muslim Golden Age

Prophet Muhammad (saw) was born in 571 C.E., in the predominantly pagan environment of Makkah, and started his mission around 610 C.E at the age of forty. After an exhausting and onerous struggle that spanned 23 years, the domination of Islam was established throughout the Arabian peninsula. Prophet Muhammad (saw) had started the process of expansion, or export, of the Islamic Revolution into the neighboring countries before his death in 632 C.E. This expansion continued unabated during the Caliphate of Abu Bakr, Umar, and Uthman (RAA), when the *Banu Isma'el* or the *Ummiyeen* gushed forth like a mighty flood, and in less than a quarter of a century Iran, Iraq, Syria Palestine Egypt, as well as a major part of North Africa came under their rule. These were the days of pure, authentic, and pristine Islam.

After a brief respite due to internal strife during the Caliphate of Ali (RAA), the process started again during the Umayyad era, and, within a short span of time, new lands were conquered that extended up to Turkestan, Afghanistan, and Sindh in the east, and included the entire North Africa and parts of Europe in the west. Spain was vanquished, and the Muslim armies reached even up to the heart of France. However, with the passage of time, the zeal of establishing the Just Social Order of Islam had started to diminish, and the element of Arab Imperialism began to dominate the Muslim conquests.

The supremacy of the Muslims reached its zenith during the 8th, 9th and 10th centuries C.E., when initially the Umayyads and then the

Abbasids held the leadership of Islam as well as that of the Muslims. Strictly speaking, however, only the Umayyad era represents the true domination of pure Arab rule, as the Abbasids were generally infected and spoiled by Persian influences. Still, during this period, *Banu Isma'el* were in ascendancy over a big chunk of land, and their culture, civilization, arts, sciences, and religion were dominant. The first three hundred years can therefore be described as the golden era of the Muslim history.

At this juncture, a point of contrast between the Muslims and the Jews becomes apparent. That is, while the first phase of rise for the Muslims began during the life time of Prophet Muhammad (saw), the corresponding period for the Jews could not start until about three hundred years after the death of Prophet Musa (AS). The reason for this difference is that the establishment of Islam as a politico-socio-economic system was achieved, at least within the boundaries of Arabian Peninsula, by Prophet Muhammad (saw) and his devoted Companions (RAA). On the other hand the Israelites, by refusing to fight for the Promised Land, had brought the revolutionary process to a halt. Hence the delay of three hundred years.

First Period of Decline

The Arabs gradually became corrupted as a result of their unprecedented power and wealth. The simple, frugal, and almost self-denying life style of the early Muslims slowly disappeared, giving way to the luxurious and hedonistic trend that is the hallmark of all worldly rulers. Due to their materialistic and this- worldly ambitions, the faith and religious enthusiasm of the Arabs faded away, leading ultimately to their political decline. Although clear signs of their hollowness and exhaustion remained shrouded for quite some time, it became increasingly obvious by the 10th century that the Arabs were reaching their senility.

During the 11th century, Arab decline and decadence became severe enough to create a power vacuum in the heart of the Muslim world. This attracted tribes from the North East, i.e., the Kurds and the Seljuk Turks, to the center of the Muslim land. These tribes, after embracing Islam, strengthened their hold in Syria, Palestine, and Egypt. This led to the infusion of fresh and energetic blood into the ailing Muslim *Ummah*. It was during this period that Afghan tribes started invading the Indian subcontinent, paving the way for the establishment of Muslim rule in India.

In the 12th and 13th centuries, the Arabs experienced their first taste of Divine punishment, and the words of the Qur'an — "We sent against you Our creatures full of martial might who ransacked your cities" — were fulfilled once again. Previously, the Jews were destroyed by the Assyrians from the North and then by the Babylonians from the East. History was repeated when the Arab Muslim were devastated first by the Crusaders from the North, and then by the Mongols from the East.

The Christian Europe launched a series of attacks, in order to recapture Jerusalem from Muslims, after Pope Urban II had declared a Holy

War in 1096 to liberate the city from "infidels." Wave after waves of Crusaders invaded the Muslim territories for the next two hundred years. During one of their initial attacks, the Crusaders conquered Jerusalem in 1099, violating the sanctity of Al-Aqsa mosque. The Christian warriors, in their extreme religious frenzy, went completely berserk after this conquest. Such wholesale butchery took place in Jerusalem that it embarrasses the Western historian even today.

The Holy City remained under Christian rule for a period of 88 years, as the decrepit Umayyads were no longer capable of launching an offensive. Finally, the fervent and zealous elements from among the non-Arab nations — under Salahuddin Ayyubi (1137-1193), an Egyptian ruler of Kurdish descent — fought successfully against the Crusaders and brought Jerusalem again under the Muslim rule in 1187. The real extermination of the Arabs, however, was still to come. Genghis Khan (1162-1227), after uniting the Mongol tribesmen, had already established a ruthless and powerful army that plundered North China, Turkestan, Transoxania, Afghanistan, and Persia. After Genghis Khan's death, his empire was divided among his sons and grandsons. The fierce Mongol warriors, however, continued to advance further east, towards the heart of Muslim land. The destruction of the romantic city of Baghdad in 1258 was brutally thorough, as most buildings were razed to the ground. For a period of forty days, the conquerors continued to massacre the inhabitants, even pregnant women were not spared. Dead bodies in street and market places were too numerous to be properly buried, leading to uncontrollable epidemics of disease which further added to the death toll. The whole social and economic framework collapsed, along with the rich traditions of culture and learning. With the execution of Mu'tasim Billah, the already flickering lamp of the Abassids

Caliphate was also extinguished.

The fall of Baghdad was not only the last episode in the first manifestation of Divine punishment to the Muslims, but it also constituted the *coupe de grâce* for the *Banu Isma'el*, as Almighty Allah (swt) sacked them from the leadership of the Muslim world. The following Qur'anic words came true, at least regarding the Arabs:

If you turn away, then Allah will bring other people in your place, who will not be like you. [TMQ Muhammad 47:38]

Life After Death

The Arabs were too severely crushed to stop the roaring and raging storm of Mongol invaders. It was the Mamluke ruler of Egypt — Saifuddin Kutuz (*Al-Malik Al-Muzaffar*) who defeated them for the first time in 1260, thereby shattering the myth of Mongol invincibility. After him, Ruknuddin Baybras inflicted several defeats on the Mongol armies, forcing them out of Syria. In this way, at least the western wing of the Muslim world was saved from destruction.

During the 12th and 13th centuries, however, the center of the Muslim land was presenting a desolate and hopeless picture. The situation there was a repetition of what had happened to Jerusalem in the 6th century B.C., when Prophet Uzair (AS) was overwhelmed with grief and had, according to the Qur'an, said to himself, *"how shall God bring this city to life after its death?"* (Al-Baqarah 2:259). But despite the widespread devastation and degradation, just as the Israelites had risen again, so did the Muslim, and the words of the Qur'an — "*Then we gave you a chance against them, and strengthened you with wealth and children, and increased your number*" (Al-Isra 17:6) — were fulfilled once again.

There was, however, a significant departure from the pattern set by the Jewish history. The previous Muslim *Ummah* was composed of a single race, and therefore their renaissance had to take place exclusively from within that race. There was no such limitation in the case of the *Ummah* of Prophet Muhammad (saw), and, as a result, the process of her revival was accomplished by the efforts of a number of non-Arab nations.

Almost miraculously, the barbaric Mongols themselves started to embrace Islam, and this provided the Muslim world with powerful defenders and guardians. Similarly, the Temurid and Ottoman Turks also converted to Islam, the former laying down the foundations of a strong Muslim dominion in India and thereby strengthening the eastern wing, and the latter establishing themselves initially in Asia Minor and then founding the Great Ottoman Empire.

The terms "Turkey" and "Ottoman Empire" are often treated as synonyms, although present-day Turkey constituted only a small part of that largest of all modern states which extended into Asia, Europe, and Africa. The capital of Byzantine or the Eastern Roman empire, Constantinople, was conquered by Muhammad II in 1453 and became the Ottoman capital. The Turks were then able to establish their domination over the whole east Europe, and also accepted the challenging and stupendous task of protecting and leading the heart of the Muslim land, including North Africa. Moreover, the institution of the Caliphate was revived and the lost greatness of the Muslims was recaptured in its totality, although this was achieved by the efforts of the Turks and not by those of the Arabs. The Ottoman empire reached its zenith under Selim I and his son Suleiman the Magnificent in the 16th century, when the Turk armies advanced through the Balkans and Hungary into Austria, and later in 1683 when they again reached up to the gates of Vienna.

Second Period of Decline

The period between 1350 and 1600 is characterized by the revival of cultural and scientific development in Europe, usually referred to as "Renaissance." It is an undeniable historical fact that this movement was triggered under the influence of the achievements of the Muslims with regard to science and scientific knowledge. The Middle Ages were, for the Christian Europe, a period of intellectual stagnation; during this period, on the other hand, the development of the scientific and inductive method among the Arab Muslims was leading to unprecedented advancement in astronomy, physics, geology, botany, medicine, and mathematics. During the time when the Christian Europe was lost in the night of ignorance, we find that Greek, Indian, and Persian sciences were being taught in the universities of Muslim Spain, attracting scholars from all over Europe. In this way, the light of reason and science reached and started to illuminate the darkness that was mediaeval Europe.

Unfortunately, the development of science and technology in Europe coincided with the downfall in Muslim political power. By now the Arab rule in Spain — established by Abdur Rahman in 750 C.E. — was in decay. Muslim Spain, therefore, became the first target of European imperialism, culminating in the fall of its last stronghold, Granada, in 1492. Today, 500 years after the decline of Muslim rule, all the magnificent architecture of the Umayyads is still standing. Muslims and the Muslim culture, however, have completely vanished from modern Spain, as if they had never existed there. Weakness, as they say, is indeed a capital crime.

In the 15th century, Prince Henry of Portugal ordered to find a sea route to India. Various expeditions were only partly successful, until Vasco da Gama became the first European explorer to finally reach India by sea, in 1497, by traveling northwards after going around the Cape of Good Hope at the southern tip of Africa. European Imperialism, which was as yet unable to colonize the Muslim lands in Asia because of the deterrence provided by the strong Ottoman Empire, was now in a position to launch her offensive through sea route. What followed was an onslaught of Portuguese, Dutch, British, and French traders-cum-conquerors, who, from 16th to 19th centuries, continued to occupy various Muslim states, exploiting all human and natural resources to their fullest. Moreover, just as the Jews were strongly influenced during the period of Greek and Roman rule by the language, culture, life-style, values, and ideas of their rulers, so were the Muslims.

By now the Ottoman Empire was in serious disarray, resulting from injustices by those in authority, decline in morality, widespread corruption, and, worst of all, lethargy and stagnation of the intelligentsia. The power vacuum created by the weakening Turks was an open invitation for the Western Imperialism to subjugate the heart of the Muslim world. And, indeed, they were only glad to oblige.

The beginning of the 20th century turned out to be the starting point for the second phase of decline in the heart of Muslim world. Thus, the British Intelligence masterminded the Arab revolt against the Turks during World War I, resulting in the segmentation of the great Ottoman Empire. Numerous smaller states were created in the Middle East and north Africa, which came under direct or indirect control of different European powers. In this way, a prediction of Prophet Muhammad (saw) came true, i.e., "There will come a time when nations of the world will invite one another to invade and exploit you, just as a person calls upon his guests to the feast" (*Abu Dawood*).

The second phase of Muslim decline reached its lowest ebb during the first quarter of the present century, when the whole of Muslim world was enslaved by the forces of Western Colonialism. Then, in 1967, the Arabs received their most ignominious defeat at the hands of a cursed nation, when the sanctity of the Al-Aqsa Mosque was violated for the second time, and the Holy City was captured by Israeli army. In this the words of the Qur'an — "When the time of the second prediction came, (We roused against you another people) to ravage you, and to enter the Temple as they had done the first time, and to destroy utterly what they conquered" (Al-Isra 17:7) — were fulfilled once again.

The most tragic and lamentable aspect of this history is the fact that the Western Imperialism had succeeded in destroying Muslim unity and their *esprit de corps*. Although Muslims were never a single political entity after the decline of the Umayyads, they still remained thoroughly connected and unified because of their common beliefs and life-style. However, the seeds of racial prejudice and nationalistic chauvinism — planted by the Western Imperialism in the beginning of the 20th century — not only weakened that sense of brotherhood and ultimately led to the winding up of Caliphate, but are still producing their bitter fruits in the form of our growing disharmony.

This malignant trend of fragmentation along ethnic, territorial, and linguistic lines has resulted in the carnage suffered by the Turks at the hands of their Arab brethren, and the massacre and utter humiliation suffered by non-Bengali Muslims at the hands of their Bengali brethren in what was then East Pakistan. The insanity of fratricide, according to the Qur'an, is one of the manifestations of Divine punishment:

Say: "He has power to send you retribution form the skies above, or the earth beneath your feet, or confound you with divisions among you, and give one the taste of the vengeance of the other." [TMQ Al- An'aam 6:65]

Back to the present

So far we have examined the similarities between the Jewish and Muslim histories vis-à-vis their two phases of rise and two phases of decline. In this context, the events of the 20th century are especially significant in that they represent — for both the Jews and the Muslims — the unfolding of the third and final stage of their respective histories.

Note that although "rise" and "decline" are essentially opposite and contradictory concepts, both of these processes are usually found simultaneously during the greater part of the history of a particular culture-civilization. In other words, both the phenomena of "rise" and "decline" may be found operating side by side, although in due course of time one of these trends gradually weakens and disappears, and the other one becomes dominant.

It is apparent to any careful observer that the Jews have continued to suffer the floggings of Divine punishment in the present century — the Holocaust during the Second World War being a case in point — just as they have been suffering for the last two thousand years. Simultaneously, however, they are also undergoing a process of revival, as exemplified by the establishment of the state of Israel. In the same way, the second phase of decline for the Muslims has continued in the present century — prominent examples of which include the termination of Ottoman Empire, abolition of the Caliphate, the Six-Day War of '67, the humiliating fall of East Pakistan, and the devastation of Iraq in the Gulf War — but, at the same time, powerful currents of revival and regeneration are also visible, as epitomized by Islamic activism throughout the world.

According to the predictions of the Qur'an and *Hadith*, the process of Muslim re-awakening and revitalization is going to continue, culminating not only in the renaissance of Islam as a moral and spiritual ideal, but also in the establishment of the Islamic System of Social Justice over the entire globe. On the other hand, the revival among the Jews is going to be evanescent and short-lived, and their continuing decline, in due course of time, will overshadow their apparent "rise," ultimately leading to their final and total extermination. Moreover, the beginning of the domination of Islam and the annihilation of the Jews will be temporally coincidental. The relevant predictions in the Qur'an and *Hadith* will be discussed later in this book. At the moment we shall consider the dynamics and details of the revival among the Muslims.

Moving Upwards

The most significant point to note in this respect is that the revival of the Muslim *Ummah* is not a simple and linear process; rather it has numerous aspects and various dimension. There are a number of devoted individuals, as well as associations, parties and organized groups, which are working diligently in different ways for Islamic revival. Although their efforts may sometime appear to be mutually conflicting, the fact remains that all of them are actually reinforcing each other vis-à-vis the overall movement for revival. Moreover, this mission of the renaissance of Islam and revitalization of the *Ummah* is not going to be completed in ten or twenty years; rather, it is a slow and patient ascent from one rung of the ladder to the next. Each and every step in this upward movement is worthy and crucial in its own right. It is possible for the work done by one's predecessors to appear trivial or even misplaced and misguided when viewed from a higher level. However, the significance and value of the contributions of the past generations cannot be easily disparaged or denied, keeping in view the specific requirements and limitations of the time and circumstances in which they were carried out. Finally, while the importance of charismatic personalities is certainly undeniable, in the final analysis they are of less value as compared to organized groups and parties. These associations, in turn, tend to lose their unique significance within the larger umbrella of particular movements, and, finally, all the different movements coalesce in the all-embracing process of revival and regeneration, which is of ultimate importance.

First stage of Revival

Strictly speaking, Islam and Muslims are two completely distinct entities, and, as such, the independence of Muslim territories from direct Western occupation should have nothing to do with the revival of Islam. However, if we are to consider this issue from a realistic perspective instead of a purely theoretical and idealistic one, the whole situation appears quite different on the ground. For all practical purposes, the future of Islam is inexorably linked with Muslim nations as they exist today, and both of them — though theoretically unrelated — are in reality dependent upon each other.

Thus, the achievement of independence and self-determination by different Muslim nations actually constitutes the first stage in the revival of Islam. Although Western domination is still very much present in the form of our intellectual, cultural, and financial enslavement, the whole Muslim land — except Palestine and Kashmir — has, by the grace of Almighty Allah (swt), succeeded in gaining freedom from direct foreign rule. Since the efforts for Islamic revival are likely to face comparatively less opposition and resistance in a country governed by Muslims as compared to the one ruled by a colonial power, it can be rightly claimed that the various movements for independence actually represented an initial stage in the process of Islamic Renaissance.

However, if it is objected that these struggles for liberation were led by people who were not, in most cases, practicing Muslims, then a saying of the Holy Prophet (saw) can explain this phenomenon. According to this prophetic saying, which is reported by Imam Bukhari, Almighty Allah (swt) sometimes chooses irreligious and grossly impious people for the service of Islam. Indeed, His plans are highly precise, yet mysterious and subtle.

We know that various regional and ethnic sentiments were invoked in order to mobilize the masses in the course of these movements for independence. Again, strictly speaking, these slogans had absolutely nothing in common with Islam. However, the degree of emotional attachment and intellectual devotion of the Muslims with Islam was certainly not strong enough for it to become the basis for a dynamic and effective movement. Under these circumstances, therefore, the use of nationalistic slogans in such movements can be justified to a large extent. In principle, it can be said that such methods are permissible only when they are used on a temporary basis — as a matter of pure expediency — and not adopted as a permanent policy. In countries where such sentiments were aroused to get rid of foreign rule, it is imperative that after the achievement of political autonomy the true Islamic spirit of Muslim unity and brotherhood be cultivated.

In this respect, the Pakistan Movement stands out as a unique and exceptional phenomenon. If the Muslims of the Indian subcontinent were to struggle against the British Raj by forming an alliance with non- Muslims on the basis of Indian Nationalism, then there was certainly enough justification to do so (and this is exactly the principle that was adopted by Jami'yat *Ulama*-e-Hind). However, what actually happened was that the overwhelming majority of Muslims based their political struggle — under the leadership of Muslim League — upon the concept of Muslim Nationhood and the Two-Nation Theory, the basis of which was neither racial or linguistic unity, nor a common homeland, but was founded upon the religious beliefs and heritage of the Muslims. This means that today there is nothing to justify the partition of British India and nothing to legitimatize our separate existence except Islam itself. It also means that Pakistan is already a step ahead of all other Muslim states by virtue of her very genesis and *raison d' être* in Muslim nationhood.

One of the most important factors which caused the Indian Muslims to define and organize themselves in terms of their religion was the prejudice and intolerance of the Hindu majority. Also, the fact that the Hindus had a burning desire to settle their old score with Muslims, and to "avenge their thousand years long humiliation," was an open secret. The ambition on the part of the Hindus to annihilate the Muslims caused the latter to wake up pretty quickly, and, in this way, the Hindus themselves paved the way for Islamic Renaissance, albeit unwittingly. Moreover, it must be kept in mind that the Indian Muslims already had an unmatched devotion and passion for Islam and the Muslim *Ummah*, as epitomized by their massive and emotional reaction at the abolition of Caliphate. Last, but not the least, was the personality of Allama Iqbal (1877-1938), whose poignant and moving poetry played a central and decisive role in awakening and invigorating the Indian Muslims from their appalling lassitude and apathy.

Second Dimension

The liberation of the Muslim states from the yoke of Western Colonialism was only the first stage in the ongoing process of Islamic revival. We now turn to the second dimension of this process, which is the role of traditional and orthodox religious scholars or *Ulama*. Numerous organizations of these *Ulama*, belonging to various schools of thought, are actively pursuing the mission of serving Islam and Muslims along the lines of their own particular methodology. In this respect too, the Indian subcontinent enjoys an outstanding and unparalleled superiority in that the grip of the *Ulama* over the masses and the popular support for the orthodox Islam in this part of the world is unmatched in the entire Muslim Land. Even the Arabian peninsula, which was dominated by the effects of the reformist movement of Muhammad Ibn Abdul Wahhab (1703-1792) up to the middle of the present century, is now too far behind the Indian subcontinent in this regard.

The reason for this phenomenon is not at all difficult to discern. A versatile and unique figure like Shah Waliyullah of Delhi (1703-1762) is not to be found anywhere else in the Muslim world during the last three hundred years. His momentous efforts in shifting the focus of Muslims away from trivial legalities and back to the original sources of Islamic faith and knowledge — the Holy Qur'an and the *Hadith* — as well as his intellectual exposition of Islamic thought and philosophy are certainly unparalleled achievements. It was Shah Waliyullah's pioneering work that had led to the enhancement of the respect for religion and religious scholars in the Indian subcontinent.

However, we must keep in mind that the main thrust of the efforts of our *Ulama* is directed only towards safeguarding and preserving the dogmatic, ritualistic, and institutional structure of Islam. As regards fulfilling the requirements and demands of reviving Islam in the present Westernized milieu, and re- establishing the ascendancy of the politico-socio-economic system of Islam, they are often unaware of even the existence of such a need. Therefore, the services of the *Ulama* can be seen as a continuation of the efforts of previous reformers of Islam, in that their efforts — like the services of present-day *Ulama* — were mainly focused on defense rather than on revival. Our noble ancestors were justified in narrowing down their fields of activity because the cultural and legal system of Islam was still very much intact in those days, and the predominant need of their time was merely to preserve the religious faith in its original form and to defend it against alien influences. As a result, all our past reformers concentrated their energies in the academic fields, or, at the most, in the moral and spiritual purification of common Muslims. None of them tried to launch any organized political or militant movement, as Prophet Muhammad (saw) had set strict restrictions on such a rebellion against Muslim rulers. According to the popular interpretation of some *Ahadith*, as long as the *Shari'ah* was being enforced and no flagrant violation of Islam was being committed, it was not considered permissible to revolt even if the rulers are themselves wicked and oppressive. Therefore, as soon as the situation changed, and non-Muslims started to conquer and occupy Muslim territories, the reformist efforts quickly turned into armed struggles. Prominent examples of this phenomenon include the *MujahiDeen* movement of Sayyid Ahmed Shaheed (1786-1831) in India, the Sanussi movement in Libya — started by Sayyid Muhammad Ibn Ali As-Sanussi

(1787-1859) — and its struggle against Italian occupation up to 1932, and the Mahdist movement — initiated by Muhammad Ahmad (1844-1885) — that resisted the British invasion in Sudan.

It is obvious that, even today, our traditional *Ulama* are following in the footsteps of earlier reformers who had worked under completely different conditions. In other words, traditional Muslim scholars have, in general, restricted themselves and their abilities within a rather narrow circle of activity, which is essentially *defensive* rather than *revivalist.* Moreover, even the task of defending Islamic doctrines is not being properly done by the *Ulama,* as they are, more often than not, completely out of touch with developments in contemporary philosophical, social, and scientific thought. Imam Ghazzali (1058-1111) and Imam Ibn Taimiyyah (1263-1328) were able to defeat the onslaught of Greek Philosophy and Aristotelian logic only after a careful and deep study of these invading ideas. Similarly, in order to deal with the modern ideologies that are seeking to destroy the foundations of Islamic faith, we need first to clearly discriminate between what is and what is not against the spirit of the Qur'an. Afterwards, we need to refute that part of the invading ideologies which is in opposition to the Qur'anic spirit, and to accept and incorporate the part that is in accordance with its spirit into a new and contemporary exposition of Islam. Unfortunately, this is not being done by our religious scholars.

The role of the *Ulama* today, instead of being that of an engine capable of propelling the ship of Islam forward, is actually nothing more than that of a heavy anchor which prevents the ship from drifting away in any wrong direction. Although, under the present circumstances, even this is a commendable and substantial service, the fact remains that this is by no means enough.

Another aspect of the activity of our *Ulama* that needs correction is their unusually strong emphasis on sectarian matters. A serious stagnation of thought along with dogmatism has set in ever since the practice of *Ijtihad* was done away with. The religious seminaries and *Ulama* of every sect are therefore spending most of their time and energies in defending and propagating their particular brands of dogma and ritual, often insisting that any variation in such matters is nothing short of apostasy. Such narrow-mindedness has exacerbated the evil of sectarianism and the resulting intolerance among the masses has led to a dangerous trend towards sectarian militancy.

One very important movement that has originated from the School of *Deoband*, the great theological seminary in India, is that of the Tablighi Jama'at, which has succeeded in causing a massive religious mobilization among the Muslims. Tablighi Jama'at has made headway in focusing the attentions of a big section of the Muslim population towards the renewal of faith. However, the overwhelming majority of the people who are being influenced by the Tablighi Jama'at are simple folks, untouched by the atheistic and materialistic philosophies of the West, and who already have a dormant inclination towards religious and moral virtue. Despite this limitation, the movement of the Tablighi Jama'at certainly occupies an important position within the larger process of Islamic Renaissance, in relation to its effort for the regeneration of faith among the masses.

Islamic Ressurgence

We are definitely indebted to the arduous and often unacknowledged efforts by our *Ulama*, as they have succeeded in keeping the structure of traditional beliefs and rituals intact during the extremely unfavorable period of Western colonialism. However, the most significant aspect of the process of our revival concerns an entirely different type of response to the decline of Muslims. The forerunners in the revivalist movement include all those organizations and groups which were created with this very purpose in mind, i.e., to re-awaken the *Ummah* and to re-establish the domination of Islam. Such groups and parties have categorically rejected the two common responses to Westernization: either withdrawing in the shells of tradition or blindly accepting whatever arrives from the West. Instead, they have emphasized again and again that Islam is not merely a collection of dogma, rituals, and customs, as are other religions, but that it is the God-given *Deen*, i.e., a complete way of life encompassing the whole spectrum of human activity, including its social, cultural, legal, economic, and political aspects. And, most importantly, like all other ways of life, Islam demands its complete and total ascendancy, and the struggle to establish that ascendancy is the duty of every Muslim

For a number of centuries, India and Egypt have held the distinction of being the two most prominent centers of culture and learning in the Muslim world. It is hardly surprising, therefore, that the two major revivalist movements of the twentieth century — Jama'at-e-Islami and Al-Ikhwan Al-Muslimun — rose from the Indian subcontinent and Egypt, respectively. Although, at a certain point in its history, the Al-Ikhwan Al- Muslimun of Egypt had become the focus of all revivalist aspirations due to its unprecedented fervor and widespread influence, the fact remains that the real superiority — in this field too — belongs to the Indian subcontinent.

The first person to invite the Muslims towards the struggle for Islamic revival in the Indian subcontinent was Maulana Abul Kalam Azad (1888-1958), who, during the early part of the present century, called for the establishment of "God's Kingdom" through his pioneering magazines *Al-Hilal* and *Al-Balagh,* and, in order to reach that goal, formed a group known as Hizbullah. His ability to motivate the audience through a unique style of writing and oratory, which became especially prominent during the Khilafat Movement, made him a well-known public figure throughout the subcontinent, and his own sincerity and enthusiasm conquered the hearts of millions of Indian Muslims. If it were not for the opposition and obstructions created by some of the traditional scholars, he would have been selected as *Imamul Hind* (supreme leader of Indian Muslims) during the early 1920s. Disillusioned and frustrated by the lukewarm response from the religious establishment, Abul Kalam gave up his mission altogether, and, from then onwards, dedicated his life to the nationalist politics of India, until his death in 1958.

The echoes of his vehement and vociferous clarion call to the Qur'an and *Jihad* continued to reverberate in the four corners of Muslim India. Like the second runner in a relay race, another unconventional and courageous young man appeared on the scene with the firm resolve to continue the mission that was forsaken by Maulana Abul Kalam. He worked alone for nearly seven years as a journalist, presenting a methodology for the establishment of "God's Kingdom" and the revival of Islam as a complete way of life. He then worked for sometime at Darul Islam — an Islamic research academy established by Chaudhry Niaz Ali Khan, a devotee of Alma Iqbal. He finally laid the foundation of his own party in 1941, called Jama'at-e-Islami, and started an organized movement. This young man was, of course, none other than Maulana Sayyid Abul A'la Maududi (1903-1979).

The spirit of Islamic revivalism and the aspiration to establish the ideal Islamic system, as generated by the Jama'at-e-Islami, has influenced a considerable section of Muslim youth in the Indo-Pakistan subcontinent. Simultaneously, the same spirit — initiated by Hassan Al-Banna when he established Al- Ikhwan Al-Muslimun in 1928 — has been active throughout most of the Arab world. Although the widespread impact produced by these movements is beyond dispute, it must be realized that lack of a unanimous policy in relation to the all important matter of methodology has been responsible for the creation of a number of divisions among them, leading to the formation of various smaller parties and organizations. For example, though the Al-Ikhwan Al-Muslimun in Egypt and Jordan has, in general, taken the path of peaceful social and political struggle, some of its dissatisfied offshoots have adopted violent and even terrorist methods for achieving the same objective.

However, such radical organizations, along with the enthusiasm of other non-violent but nevertheless revolutionary groups, have succeeded in bringing the goal of Islamic Resurgence a bit closer to reality — atleast in the eyes of the West. The whole phenomenon has produced a sense of alarm among the Western powers and their "Muslim" stooges, despite the fact that the actual achievements of parties like Takfir-wal- Hijra, Al-Jehad, Islamic Tendency Society, Jama'a Islamia, Hizb-ut-Tahrir, and Islamic Salvation

Front (FIS), are as yet far from the establishment of an Islamic state. One can have a number of disagreements with each of these organizations, but it has to be admitted that these movements represent, as a whole, the revivalist aspirations of the Muslim *Ummah*, and have become a force that has to be recognized at the international level. The role of the revolution in Iran and the rise of Shi'ite fundamentalism is also significant in this respect.

Jewish Revival

As mentioned before, the beginning of the third and final phase of rise for the Muslims is coincidental with the temporary upswing of the Jews. It can be seen that, at the present moment, the upward trend in the history of the Muslim *Ummah* is not only very slow and gradual, but that it is still in its initial stages. On the other hand, the same trend among the Jews not only started much earlier, but that it has shown a far more rapid and swift progress. Thus, the ingenious scheme prepared by the "Elders of Zion" in 1897, and the political Zionism of Theodore Herzel (1860-1904), bore fruit within a short period of twenty years, resulting in the Balfour Declaration by the British Government on November 2, 1927, that paved the way for the "establishment in Palestine of a national home for the Jewish people." Finally, the illegitimate state of Israel was born on May 14, 1948, with the British Government acting as midwife.

The situation at the moment is that not only Israel herself is a formidable military power, but the entire Western world is also there to support and patronize her, both economically and with respect to arms supply. The "Supreme Power" of our time — the United States of America — is practically in the tight grip of a small Jewish minority, who is able to exert an immense amount of control over its international policies. This last mentioned fact has been forcefully proved by former US Congressman Paul Findley, in his best- selling book *They Dare to Speak Out.* More importantly, the global financial system is virtually in the hands of Jewish bankers, who, through the institution of interest or usury, have become powerful enough to command the obedience of entire governments. Finally, the monarchs and rulers in most of the Arab countries have either made their peace with

Israel or are desperately looking for opportunities to demonstrate their servile acquiescence. It seems, therefore, that there is no power on earth that can prevent the establishment of "Greater Israel."

Under these apparently hopeless circumstances only the predictions of the Holy Qur'an and *Hadith* can reassure us. According to these predictions, the third phase of rise for the Muslims will be accompanied by the global domination of Islam, which will last till near the end of the world, whereas the present rise of the Jews is going to be ephemeral. Moreover, as mentioned before, the conflict between the Jews and the Muslims is going to result, ultimately, in the total extermination of the former, according to the Divine law of "annihilation of the worst." However, the most significant role in this conflict — which is gradually warming up to its grand finale — is going to be played by a third power, the Christians.

Third of the Trinity – The Christian

An interesting theme that is common to all pagan religions is the idea of "henotheism"; wherever there was a group of people that worshipped a number of divine beings, we find that there was always a Supreme Deity that was considered to be above all other gods and goddesses. This trend is most prominent in Hinduism, in the Greek and Roman mythologies, and among the pagan Arabs of the pre-Islamic era. However, what is really important to note in such religions is that, in actual practice, the smaller gods and goddesses always get the lion's share in the attention and devotion of their worshipers, while the Supreme God disappears in the background, as He is carelessly ignored and casually brushed aside by the worshipers.

Applying this analogy to the three Abrahamic faiths, we can say that although Christianity is the biggest among them in terms of the number of adherents, yet in reality — except for the name and personality of Prophet Isa (AS) — there is hardly any thing in this religion that can be described as "Christian." That is to say, the doctrines and practices of Christianity, as they exist toady, have more to do with the innovations of St. Paul than with the real teachings of Prophet Isa (AS). As such, the present-day Christianity actually belongs to the realm of philosophical religions — along with Hinduism, Taoism, and Confucianism — instead of the domain of Revealed religions like Judaism and Islam.

Coming back to the original topic of our discussion, it is significant to note that the Christian nations have played a crucial role vis-à-vis the second phase of decline with regard to both the Jews and the Muslims. Thus, we find that the torture, persecution, genocidal killings, and exile suffered by the Jews during the last sixteen hundred years were caused exclusively by the Christians. Ever since the conversion of Romans to Christianity in the fourth century C.E., Jews have continuously been made the target of various allegations, and executed by the thousands on one pretext or the other. Similarly, it was the Christians who were responsible for the brutal massacre suffered by the Muslims during the Crusades, and then the subjugation and exploitation of the Muslims at the hands of Western Imperialism. From even a superficial survey of Jewish and Muslim histories, therefore, it becomes clear that Almighty Allah (swt) has been using the Christian nations as an instrument of His punishment, or the whip of His retribution, for both the Jews and Muslims of the world.

However — and this is vital for us to keep in mind — there has been a profound metamorphosis in the nature of the relationship between the Jews and Christians; this change has started from the days of the Renaissance, reaching its climax only during the present century. As a result of this change, the Christian world — particularly the White Angle-Saxon Protestants or WASP — have become devoted comrades and staunch supporters of the Jewish nation, although they are, in fact, only being cleverly used and manipulated by the latter. On the other hand, the highly ruthless historical role of the Christians in relation to the Muslim *Ummah* is still very much intact. As such, there is a clear possibility of another massive assault, a 'la Crusades, that can work havoc upon the Muslims, particularly the Arab world. Such an event can obviously result in killings and destruction on a huge scale, a minor glimpse of which has already been witnessed by the world during the Operation Desert Storm.

The way in which the "threat" of militant and fundamentalist Islam is being hyperbolized by the Western media betrays an attempt to create public hatred against the Muslims, as was done before and during the Crusades. This process of brainwashing is exemplified, at the popular level, by the PBS documentary *Jihad in America* and the Reader's Digest article A *Holy War Heads Our Way*; prominent examples of the same trend at an intellectual level include *The Clash of Civilizations* by Samuel P. Huntington and *The Roots of Muslim Rage* by Bernard Lewis. Similarly, a campaign was recently launched in the Western media so as to inculcate the notion, with reference to the writings of Nostradamus, that the "Anti-Christ" is going to be a Muslim leader from among the Arabs.

The very idea of Muslims going back to their roots — the Holy Qur'an and the *Sunnah* of Prophet Muhammad (saw) — is being depicted as a dangerous combination of extremism, terrorism, and fanaticism. Unfortunately, after the end of Cold War and the demise of Communism, Islam and Muslims are increasingly being used to fill the vacuum of the "Great Menace" against which the West can test her powers. With ever rising zeal, Islamic fundamentalism is being portrayed as the ultimate evil against which the forces of decency must unite. Despite this continuing campaign of disinformation about the horrible hazard of Islam, the fact remains that, in the history of Muslim-Christian relationship, it was always the Muslims who suffered heavily at the hands of various Christian nations and not the other way round. It appears that the history might repeat itself in the form of a real clash of civilizations.

ABC of Christianity

According to the Qur'an, there has been only one true religion throughout human history, i.e., Islam; all other systems of belief and worship, as they exist today, are nothing but corrupted and distorted replicas of the originally pure and simple teachings of the various messengers of God. Most versions of these teachings have been perverted beyond recognition, and the historical continuity and doctrinal similarity of only two of them — Judaism and Christianity — can at present be linked with Islam. Among these three major faiths, as mentioned earlier, only the followers of Judaism and Islam can be described as *Ummahs*: Jews or the Israelites as the previous Muslim *Ummah*, and the followers of Prophet Muhammad (saw) as the present and final Muslim *Ummah*. According to the prophecies as they appear in the *Hadith* literature, the ultimate conflict of the future is going to take place between the Jews and the Muslims, although a very significant initial role will be played by the Christian nations. In order to correctly interpret and fully comprehend these prophecies, it is imperative for us to understand the nature and history of Christian faith.

A set of three doctrines is common to the followers of most of the Christian denomination, viz., the Trinity, Crucifixion of Jesus Christ, and Atonement. The most basic creed of modern Christianity is, of course, the belief that God is one, in three persons, and in one substance: God the father, God the son, and God the Holy Spirit are not three gods, but one God. The Holy Qur'an emphatically rejects and condemns this polytheistic view.

O People of the Book, do not be fanatical in your faith, and say nothing but the truth about God. The Messiah who is Isa, son of Maryum, was only a messenger of God, and a command of His which He sent to Maryum, as a mercy from Him.

So believe in God and His messengers, and do not say "Three." For God is only one God. [TMQ Al- Nisa 4:171]

They are surely infidels who say: "God is the Messiah, son of Maryum." ...Disbelievers are they surely who say: "God is the third of the Trinity"; but there is no god other than God the One. [TMQ Al-Ma'ida 5:72,73]

The Holy Qur'an also repudiates their belief that Prophet Isa (AS) was humiliated and executed on the cross, and thus indirectly refutes the theory of Atonement — the belief that the great sacrifice from the so-called "Son of God" was necessary to remove the burden of the Original Sin from the shoulders of humanity. According to the Qur'an:

And (the Jews were punished, among other things, because) of saying, "We killed the Messiah, Isa, son of Maryum." — who was a Messenger of God — but they neither killed nor crucified him. though it so appeared to them. They have no knowledge about it, other than conjecture, and surely they did not kill him. [TMQ Al-Nisa 4:157]

Although the myth of the Crucifixion of Prophet Isa (AS) is narrated in all the four Gospels, there is absolutely no substance whatsoever in them for the doctrine of Trinity or that of the Divine Sonship of Jesus. The earliest evidence of the last two doctrines first appeared in the writings of St. Paul, and these were adopted as official beliefs of Christianity only after extensive debate, and following a long-standing controversy which included, at times, violent episodes between Unitarians and Trinitarians. These dogmas were confirmed as official beliefs of the Church, after much deliberation, during the Council of Nicaea in 325 C.E., almost three centuries after the departure of Prophet Isa (AS).

Five points of Convergence

As far as the personality of Prophet Isa (AS) is concerned, we find that there are at least five significant points which are common between the Holy Qur'an and the *Hadith* on the one hand, and the four Canonical Gospels on the other. It is indeed significant that more than half of the world's population is in agreement regarding these points, three of which are in clear opposition to the normal physical laws of the universe. We shall discuss these points one by one.

(1) The Gospel of Matthew (1:18-24) and Luke (1:26-38) mention that Jesus Christ was conceived without a human father, as a miracle from Almighty God; so does the Holy Qur'an (Aal-e-Imran 3:45-47 & Maryum 19:17-21)

(2) Jesus Christ performed the most astonishing of miracles — unparalleled in the history of Prophethood with respect to their unambiguous and unmistakable nature. These miracles are described in various sections of the Gospels (see, for example, Matthew, Chapters 8 & 14) as well as in the Holy Qur'an (Aal-e-Imran 3:49 & Al-Ma'ida 5:110)

(3) Jesus Christ forcefully and incisively called upon his fellow Israelites to mend their perverted ways, to give up sinful and unethical practices, to repent with the true spirit of repentance, and to purify themselves from all spiritual and moral corruption. He severely criticized the pretentious religiosity, the emphasis on hollow but legally spotless rituals, and the servile adherence to the letter of the law with no regard to its spirit — the hallmark of the religious establishment of his time.

(Matthew 23, and the Holy Qur'an Al-Ma'ida 5:78). As a result, he became the sole target of the acrimony and malevolence from the rabbis, the priests, and the pharisees.

(4) The message and proclamation of Jesus Christ attracted the attention of the population both in and around Jerusalem, but it was accepted only by a very minute section of the Jews, of which even fewer became his dedicated companions. The number of these close comrades, according to the Gospels, was twelve, although the matter of their names is controversial.

(5) Jesus Christ was raised up alive from the earth, and he will reappear some time before the end of the world. This has been mentioned in Matthew 28:6,7; Mark 16:19; Luke 24:51, John 20:17. Ascension and reappearance of Prophet Isa (AS) has also been alluded to in the Holy Qur'an (Al-Nisa 4:157, 158 and Al- Zukhruf 43:61), but these hints are explained more explicitly in the *Hadith*.

Innovations by Paul

Then we have two very important points, regarding which the Qur'an and *Hadith* as well as the four Gospels are unanimous, but which have been radically changed by St. Paul during the period immediately following the departure of Prophet Isa (AS). These innovations have transformed what was only a reform movement among the Jews into a philosophical religion full of pagan conceptions.

(1) It is abundantly clear from Matthew 5:17-19, Luke 16:17 and Mark 13:31, that Jesus Christ had no intention whatsoever to give any new law, nor to rescind and abolish the Mosaic law, as he was sent by Almighty God only to renew and reinforce the law of the Torah, to purify his people from spiritual and moral degeneration, and to revive the authentic spirit of *Deen*. He was, obviously, one of the Jews and was not supposed to become the founder of a new religion and a new community. However, preaching in the name of Jesus Christ, the actual founder of Christianity, St. Paul, simply abrogated the Mosaic law (Romans 4:15). The historian Michael Hart has the following to say in his book "The Hundred":

Paul, more than any other man, was responsible for the transformation of Christianity from a Jewish sect into a world religion. His central ideas of the divinity of Christ and of justification by faith alone have remained basic to Christian thought throughout all the intervening centuries ... Indeed, the influence of Paul's ideas has been so great that some scholars have claimed that he, rather than Jesus, should be regarded as the principal founder of the Christian religion.

(2) According to the Holy Qur'an, Prophet Isa (AS) was appointed a prophet only for the Israelites (Aal-e-Imran 3:49 & Al-Saff 61:6), and this

is confirmed by his sayings which appear in the Gospels (Matthew 10:5,6 & 15:24), where he forbids his disciples from extending their evangelistic activity outside that circle. However, a controversial step was taken in this respect by St. Paul, who persuaded the small number of early followers of Prophet Isa (AS) — after a period of serious dispute — to preach among the non-Jews as well. As it happened, Paul had met with little success among the Israelites, but his sweeping innovations made the new faith much more palatable for the neighboring pagan people, and thus his brand of Christianity rapidly gained popularity among these nations.

The Myth of Crucifixion

Last, but not the least, is the matter of the alleged crucifixion of Prophet Isa (AS), regarding which there is a crucial disagreement between the Islamic belief and the account of the four Canonical Gospels. According to the latter, the supreme Jewish authority in Roman Palestine — the Sanhedrin — convicted Jesus of blasphemy and insisted for death sentence, which was carried out by the Roman governor Pilate Pontius by way of crucifixion. Afterwards, on the third day, the dead body of Jesus Christ was miraculously resurrected and revived; the Christ then met with his disciples, and, after giving them some instructions, ascended into the heaven.

On the other hand, the Holy Qur'an strongly rejects the idea of Prophet Isa (AS) having been crucified, and — according to the authentic Prophetic traditions or *Hadith* — he was saved from such an accursed and humiliating death by direct Divine intervention and raised up alive into the heavens. It has also been unequivocally explained to us by Prophet Muhammad (saw) that Prophet Isa (AS) will reappear on earth to live out the rest of his life, and then he will die like any other mortal.

The only void left in this Islamic tradition, however, concerns the "when" and "where" of the ascension of Prophet Isa (AS), and the question regarding "who" actually got crucified in his place. This vacuum can be satisfactorily filled with the help of the narration in the "Gospel of Barnabas" according to which, when the traitor Judas Iscariot came ahead of the Roman soldiers and entered the garden where Prophet Jesus Christ was hiding, God the Almighty caused his face and voice to be changed so that he looked and talked exactly like Jesus, while in the meantime the prophet himself was raised up into the heavens. Thus it was the traitor who was crucified, while Prophet Jesus Christ was miraculously saved by direct

Divine intervention. It may be pointed out here that, unlike Barnabas who was a close disciple and companion of Prophet Jesus, none of the writers of the four so-called authentic gospels — i.e., Matthew, Mark, Luke, or John — ever met with the prophet himself. These gospels were written between 70 C.E and 115 C.E. but their earliest available manuscripts date back to the fourth century C.E, making their authenticity rather dubious. A number of different gospels were in circulation throughout the early period of Christianity, the manuscripts of which were freely altered and amended by the copyists in order to suit the doctrines of their particular sect. The four gospels that are included in the New Testament were accepted as genuine by the Church — and the rest were rejected as apocryphal, and their possession prohibited — not on the basis of merit, but only because these four books were in conformity with the official Church dogma. The Gospel of Barnabas was among the books that were banned in 325 C.E by the Nicean Council; it was forbidden by the Decree of the Western Churches in 382 C.E; it was again banned by Pope Innocent in 465 C.E, and then by the Glasian Decree in 496 C.E. To this day, Christian authorities refuse to accept the Gospel of Barnabas as authentic, despite striking similarities between this Gospel and the documents discovered in 1947 in the caves of Qumran, popularly called the Dead Sea Scrolls. This is because the Gospel of Barnabas proclaims absolute Divine Unity, criticizes the pagan innovations of St. Paul, declares the truth about the myth of Crucifixion, and, above all, contains unambiguous prophecies regarding the advent of Prophet Mohammad (saw), all of which is enough to destroy the very foundations of the Christian faith as it exists today. However, any unbiased comparative study of the New Testament, the Dead Sea Scrolls, and the Gospel of Barnabas is bound to reveal that this gospel is the correct and genuine account of the life and teachings of Prophet Isa (AS), notwithstanding the flimsy objections being raised by the Christians.

Allies of one another

The early Christians were generally considered as nothing more than a Jewish sect, but with the passage of time the alien concepts implanted by St. Paul — Trinity, Atonement, Abolition of the Mosaic Law — made them a different people altogether. The initial three centuries of the Common Era were characterized by severe persecution being inflicted upon the Christians, a considerable segment of which still consisted of Unitarians, at the hands of both the Jews and the Romans. However, the whole situation changed dramatically when the Roman Empire embraced Christianity, as a result of which the Jews became the target of official harassment and oppression. As the Christians saw it, Jews were guilty of "deicide," the murder of their God, and therefore they excluded the latter from the mainstream of socio-economic life. This trend continued unabated in the Middle Ages, often manifiesting as wholesale killings of the Jews. In 1096, for example, the Crusaders on their way through France and Germany massacred thousands of Jews. Widespread killings took place in 1146 by the armies of the second Crusade. More than a thousand Jews were hanged in England, in 1234, for allegedly circumcising a Christian boy. In 1290, Jews were banished from England by King Edward. In 1350, they were held responsible for the spread of plague, and hundreds of thousands were murdered in Europe. They were forced to live together under subhuman conditions called "Ghettos." Religious courts, or "Inquisition," ordered the burning of thousands of Jews during the 15th century, and these events were witnessed and celebrated as popular holidays.

Ironically enough, during more than a thousand years of humiliation and persecution, the only respite of peace and prosperity enjoyed by the Jews was in the Muslim territories. Jewish historians like Abba Eban and Solomon Grayzel have acknowledged and recognized their "Golden Age of Diaspora" — the period of Jewish affluence and growth in Muslim Spain. When the Arab rule came to end in 1492, and the Jews were immediately expelled from Spain by the Christian rulers Ferdinand and Isabella, they were given refuge and asylum in the Ottoman Empire. Large population of Jews continued to prosper peacefully in Iraq, Syria, Yemen, and Egypt, during the time when their brethren were suffering miserably in Europe, particularly in the Russian lands.

According to the Holy Qur'an, the hatred and enmity between the Jews and the Christians will last till the end of the world (Al-Ma'ida 5:14 & 64). However, we can clearly see that their mutual rancor underwent a very slow and gradual decline during the last few hundred years. The Qur'an seems to be saying, therefore, that the present coalition between the Jews and the Christians is only superficial and cosmetic as well as transient, and also that the end of the world is not very far.

We know that the Jews had always viewed themselves as a special breed of people, superior to the rest of the humanity as the "Chosen People of the Lord," who are born to rule the Gentiles. As a result, they couldn't come to terms with their shockingly unexpected humiliation, and thus the episodes of Divine retribution — instead of softening their hearts and producing in them a desire to repent and the willingness to atone for their collective crimes — has produced in them a revengeful and malicious envy and a sort of diabolical bitterness.

It would of course be unfair to make sweeping generalizations because individual persons vary greatly, but as far as the collective psyche of the Jewish nation is concerned, it is undeniable that they have developed a deeply ingrained tendency to conspire and to maneuver things surreptitiously for their own gain, without ever appearing on the stage. It may be pointed out that this character of the Jews was already prominent during the days of Prophet Muhammad (saw), and that it is this very inclination towards behind- the-scene subversive activities that has produced the present state of alliance and so-called friendship between them and the Christians.

The persecuted Jews were well aware that the only way to turn the table on their arch enemy, the Christians, was by way of minimizing the influence of religion over them and by debilitating the authority of the Church. Thus, they ingeniously used the spirit of rationalism — that was already spreading form Muslim Spain into Christian Europe — to make a breach in the bastion of Christian faith. As a matter of fact, the highly irrational and almost ridiculously illogical dogmas being enforced by the Church in the name of religion were never in a position to stand against the tide of Reason. The Renaissance in Europe was characterized by an intense interest in the physical world and in the knowledge derived from concrete sensory experience, and a decline in metaphysical beliefs and interest in the life after death, both of which were prominent themes during the Middle Ages. This rise of Reason, therefore, turned out to be the beginning of the end for Christianity and the onset of the domination of materialism and pragmatic morality. The European Jews — by playing a key role in polluting the essence of rationalism with the evils of licentiousness and promiscuity, as well as with that of intellectual vagrancy which is euphemistically called "liberalism" — were able to increase their influence in the Christian society. The rise of sexual permissiveness and the resulting breakdown of traditional family values in the West represents only one aspect of the defeat of Christian morality against the financial interests and the growing influence of the Jews.

At the same time, the rise of Protestantism and the movement for "Reformation" opened the gates of unlimited individual freedom and destroyed the unity of Christendom. Although usurious money-lending activity of the Jews had existed on a small scale throughout the middle Ages, the weakening of the Church, along with the liberal views of John Calvin (1509-1594) in Economics, ultimately led to an enormous rise in the previously prohibited practice of usury. The acceptance by the Christians that such transactions are unavoidable for economic growth and material prosperity made them willing hostages of the money-lending institutions — banks, insurance companies, stock exchanges and the like — all of which were, and still are, strongholds of the Jewish people. Today these financial institutions are the uncontested rulers of the Western World, particularly of Great Britain and the United States. The introduction of paper money instead of gold and silver has also greatly bolstered this wicked web of control and exploitation. This is how the Jews were able to take control of the affairs of the world without really exposing or endangering themselves.

This unnatural and artificial alliance between the Jews and the Christians — the basis of the so- called New World Order — is actually nothing more than the relationship between a parasite and its host, or between a master and his slave. One of the recent manifestations of this bizzare friendship is the decree issued by the Pope, exonerating the Jews from the two-thousand years old charge of crucifying Jesus Christ. The Holy Qur'an had prophetically warned us of the dangers of this coalition thus:

O Believers, do not hold Jews and Christians as your allies. They are allies of one another; and anyone who makes them his friends is surely one of them; and God does not guide the unjust. (Al-Ma'ida 5:51)

Before the Doomsday

It is an essential part of our faith as Muslims that we take the universe in which we live as created and contingent and not eternal. Unlike the early Greeks, who thought that the universe had always existed, the Holy Qur'an teaches us that ours is a very large but finite universe in terms of both space and time, and as such it has a definite beginning and a certain end. The following scenario emerges when we study modern cosmology from an Islamic perspective.

In the beginning, Almighty Allah (swt) created a concentrated core of light-energy, and then, later on, He caused it to explode in a Big Bang, leading to the creation of time, space, and matter. This phenomenon of creation out of nothing represents the manifestation of divine command "Be!" The Big Bang did not happen at any specific place, as the "space" itself was created with this explosion. Similarly, it did not occur at any particular instant, as the "time" itself came into being with the Big Bang.

Since then, the universe has been continuously expanding, rotating, and evolving. At a predetermined point in the future, it will stop expanding, and from then on the contraction or folding-back phase of the universe will commence — either due to the gravitational pull of the unseen matter exceeding the forces of expansion, or as a result of the swallowing up of entire galaxies by Black Holes — leading ultimately to the Big Crunch, which is the disappearance of the cosmos in a catastrophic implosion, like the Big Bang in reverse.

The Big Crunch will be followed by another Big Bang, leading to the creation of a new universe that will last forever, and which will be totally different from our present universe, utterly beyond the realm of our imagination. We believe, on the authority of the Qur'an and Prophet Muhammad (saw), in the rebirth of all humanity, their final judgment, the Hell and the Paradise, though the exact nature of that state of existence is simply inconceivable.

As far as the end of our own world is concerned, it seems that a major catastrophe will befall, destroying a part of our galaxy including the sun and the earth, and that this will happen well before the universal doomsday or the Big Crunch. It is this local doomsday that is referred to in the Holy Qur'an as the "Startling Calamity" or the "Inevitable."

The Ascendancy of Islam

There are a few cryptic remarks in the Holy Qur'an regarding the events which will precede the Doomsday; these points are fully explained in the form of detailed prophecies that appear in the traditions of Prophet Muhammad (saw). According to these prophecies four major events will happen before the end of the world; in chronological sequence, they are as follows:

1. The Ultimate World War of human history, which will be fought predominantly in the Middle East;
2. The appearance of Anti-Christ, or Dajjal, in the final phase of that war — a leader who will inflict huge sufferings and destruction on Arab Muslims;
3. The reappearance of Prophet Isa (AS), who will cause the extermination of Dajjal and his Jewish followers; and finally,
4. The establishment of the system of *Khilafah*, or the domination of Islam, over the entire globe.

Except for the reappearance of Prophet Isa (AS), there is nothing supernatural or incredible in these prophecies, as we shall discuss shortly. The very idea of the global domination of Islam however, seems like a fool's fantasy, keeping in view the present state of humiliation of the Muslims and their virtual enslavement by the New World Order.

Under the existing state of affairs, which is both distressing and disheartening, we must keep on reminding ourselves that the ascendancy of Islam over the entire globe is bound to come, as this has been emphatically foretold by none other than the Last Messenger of Allah (swt) himself, may

Allah's peace and blessings be upon him. Although there is no such explicit and unequivocal guarantee in the Holy Qur'an, we find that both the minor and major premises of this syllogism are repeatedly mentioned, the inescapable conclusion of which is the ultimate establishment of world-wide supremacy of Islam. The major premise consists of the fact that Prophet Muhammad (saw) was appointed a messenger and envoy of Almighty Allah (swt) for the whole humanity (Al-Qur'an Al-A'raaf 7:158; Al-Anbia 21:107; Al-Furqan 25:1; Saba 34:28; & Al-Jum'ah 62:2,3), whereas the minor premise is represented by the Divine assertion that the true way of life or *Deen al-Haq* will be made superior over the entire system of life (Al-Taubah 9:33; Al-Fath 48:24; & Al-Saff 61:9), and that God the Almighty is going to perfect His Light despite all the resistance from the unbelievers (Al-Taubah 9:32 & Al-Saff 61:8).

The logical conclusion that necessarily follows from these premises is that the real purpose and the ultimate aim of the advent of Prophet Muhammad (saw) will be fulfilled only with the establishment of the ascendancy of Islam over the entire mankind, all over the world. This has been promised by Almighty Allah (swt) in these words:

God has promised that He will surely make those of you who believe and do the right, vicegerents in the land, as He had made those before them, and He will surely establish their *Deen* which He has chosen for them, and He will surely change their state of fear into peace and security. (Al-Noor 24:55)

The Ascent of Humanity

The global domination of Islam also appears inevitable in the context of the idea of cosmic evolution, as explained in the following paragraphs:

In sharp contrast to all the materialistic theories of modern science, the Holy Qur'an teaches us that Allah (swt) is the only real force behind every creative activity that takes place in the universe. The clear and obvious signs of purpose and direction in the cosmos indicate that there is an intelligent mind at work, as pure chance could only have produced total chaos. The cosmic existence, as the Holy Qur'an proclaims again and again, is something profoundly meaningful. The evolution of the universe in the direction of a predetermined goal is what provides everything with a single grand purpose. The universe is continuously in a process of evolution, constantly working to perfect itself.

According to Dr. Muhammad Rafiuddin (whose philosophy of history was mentioned earlier), the cause of the evolution of cosmos is the desire or the will of the Creator. This desire or will of Allah (swt) is flowing in the universe as a current of consciousness, changing the universe with a view to bringing it to the stage of its highest perfection. This cosmic evolution can be described as taking place in several stages, as follows:

The first stage was that of *physical* evolution, from the Big Bang up to the time when simple chemical compounds grew into complex organic molecules, leading to the emergence of life on earth. This stage of purely physical change was directed by the Divine current of consciousness that continuously runs through all matter, causing it to behave in specific ways, commonly known as the "laws of nature."

The second stage was that of *biological* evolution, when the same current of consciousness took the form of an indwelling life-force (compare Bergson's *élan vital*), which directed the process towards the creation of the perfect animal, the Homo sapiens. It has been theorized on the basis of the pointers in the Holy Qur'an that, at this stage, Almighty Allah (swt) selected a single pair of these human-animals, and endowed them with their spiritual souls; this was the creation of Adam and Eve, the primordial human pair.

The third stage was that of *intellectual* evolution, when the current of consciousness took the form of an urge for Beauty and Perfection, expressing itself in the love of an ideal (compare Freud's *Libido*), guiding the process towards the climax of intellectual and psychological development, that was finally achieved in the personality of Prophet Ibrahim (AS).

The fourth stage was that of the collective *social* evolution of humanity, reaching its zenith in the life and teachings of Prophet Muhammad (saw), when the true way of life or *Deen al-Huq* was perfected and the ideal system of social, economic, and political Justice was presented to the mankind in its final form.

At the present moment, humanity is passing through the final stage of its evolution. The Divine current of consciousness is still active in the collective mind of humanity, urging and guiding us towards the ultimate state of human perfection, i.e., towards the establishment of the global culture-civilization that will be based upon the teachings of the Qur'an. In this way the philosophy of Ideals, as developed by Dr. Muhammad Rafiuddin, makes it even more understandable how the global domination of Islam before the end of the world is inevitable from an evolutionary stand point.

This global domination of Islam has been clearly predicted in the sayings of Prophet Muhammad (saw), three of which are quoted below:

(1) According to a tradition that is narrated by Imam Ahmad (RA) on the authority of Nauman Ibn Bashir (RAA), Prophet Muhammad (saw) is reported to have said to his Companions: "The period of Prophethood will remain among you so long as Allah wills, then He shall cause it to end. After that, there will be *Khilafah* among you on the pattern of Prophethood, and this will last as long as Allah wills, and then He shall cause it to end. After that, there will be a reign of oppressive monarchy, and this will also last as long as Allah wills, and then He shall cause it to end. After that there will be a period of enslavement, and this will last as long as Allah wills, then He shall cause it to end. Finally, there will again be *Khilafah* on the pattern ofProphethood."

(2) In another tradition narrated by Imam Muslim (RA) on the authority of Thauban (RAA), the Prophet Muhammad (saw) is reported to have said: "Allah (swt) folded up the whole earth for me (in a vision), so that I was able to see all the easts and all the wests, and surely the domination of my followers will be established over all those places that were shown to me by thus folding the earth."

(3) Imam Ahmad (RA) has narrated, on the authority of Miqdad Ibn Aswad (RAA), that the Prophet of God (saw) is reported to have said: "There shall be no house on the entire earth — neither of bricks nor one made of camel's skin — but Allah (swt) will cause the word of Islam to enter it, either with the honor of the one who deserves honor, or with the subjugation of the one who is defeated." (That is to say, God will confer

honor on some and they will embrace Islam, and He will cause the others to give up fighting and they will surrender before the rule of Islam.) ****

The way to Gods kingdom

Belief in the most certain event of Doomsday is part of our faith as Muslims, and, in this context, the global happenings of our age clearly indicate that the end of the world is probably a matter of near future.

This opinion is based upon the predictions of Prophet Muhammad (saw), many of which have already come true in the world around us, and the stage is obviously being set for the final set of events before Doomsday — the grand finale of the global drama. We shall now discuss these coming events which will precede the establishment of the domination of Islam, as disclosed by Prophet Muhammad (saw).

Indications regarding the greatest World War of human history that appear in the *Hadith* collections are, in general, couched in allegorical language. It seems that The War will take place in three phases, and will be fought predominantly in the Middle East. During the first phase, Muslim and Christian armies will join hands and fight against a third force, the identity of which is uncertain. The allies will defeat their common enemy, but then serious discord and hostility will break out between them, leading to the second phase of The War characterized by fierce fighting between the Muslim and Christian armies. Initially the Christians will have the upper hand, and the Muslims will lose important strongholds like Turkey, Lebanon, Syria, and Iraq. Although during the first and second phases the Jews themselves will not take part in the battle, their resources, technical know-how, and their propaganda machinery will be used with utmost destructive effect against the Muslims.

According to the prophecies, at this point the Muslims will select a rightly guided man as their military and political leader. This leader, called Mahdi in *Hadith* literature, will reorganize and unite the Muslim forces against the Christians, shifting the fortunes of The War in favor of the Muslims.

The third phase of The War will commence with the appearance on the scene of an exceedingly cunning Jewish leader — Dajjal or Anti-Christ. From then onwards the Jews will start to take active part in the fighting, and the combined forces of Jews and Christians will inflict heavy losses on the Muslims. At this stage — Prophet Muhammad (saw) has told in unequivocal words — Prophet Isa (AS) will reappear to strengthen and reinforce the Muslim armies. He will deliver the final installment of Divine punishment to the Jews, and will kill their leader, Dajjal. The reappearance of Prophet Isa (AS) will mark the end of Christianity as a separate religion, and the most glorious and peaceful era of human history will commence. This will be "God's Kingdom on earth," when the *Deen* of Allah (swt) will reign supreme, and the world will enjoy unprecedented bounties and blessings of the Lord.

This period of *Khilafah* on the pattern of Prophethood will last so long as Almighty Allah (swt) wills; then, after this blissful era, the world will once again be filled with wickedness. All the faithful population of the world will die peacefully and calmly one day, just before the end of the world. In this way, only the unbelievers and the wicked shall be left to face the dreadful events of the Doomsday.

Armageddon!

It is interesting to note that prophecies regarding an ultimate World War between the forces of Good and the forces of Evil are also found in the Christian tradition. The highly cryptic and symbolic language of the last book in the New Testament — the Revelations of John — is often difficult to interpret, but the references to the beast and the false prophet resembles closely the Muslim concept of Dajjal; the woman riding the beast most probably refers to the Jews and their revival; the rider coming on the white horse seems like representing the Second Coming of Prophet Isa (AS). Here are a few excerpts:

I saw three foul spirits like frogs coming from the mouths of the dragon, the beast, and the false prophet. These are demonic spirits with power to work out miracles, sent out to muster all the kings of the world for the battle on the great day of God the sovereign Lord. (16:13,14)

...I saw a woman mounted on a scarlet beast which was covered with blasphemous names and had seven heads and ten horns... I saw that the woman was drunk with the blood of God's people, and with the blood of those who had borne their testimony to Jesus... the angel said... the beast you saw was once alive, and it is alive no longer, but has yet to ascend out of the abyss before going to be destroyed. (17:3,6-8)

I saw heaven wide open, and a white horse appeared; its rider's name was Faithful and True, for he is just in judgment and just in war... The armies of heaven followed him... Out of his mouth came a sharp sword to smite the nation; for it is he who will rule them with a rod of iron... I saw the beast and the kings of the earth with their armies mustered to do battle against the rider and his army. The beast was taken prisoner, along with the false prophet who has worked miracles in its presence and deluded those who had received the mark of the beast and worshipped its image. The two of them were thrown alive into the lake of fire with its sulfurous flames. The rest were killed by the sword which came out of the rider's mouth, and the birds all gorged themselves on their flesh (19:11,14,15,19-21)

I saw an angel coming down from heaven with the key to the abyss and a great chain in his hand. He seized the dragon, that ancient serpent who is the Devil, or Satan, and chained him up for a thousand years; he threw him into the abyss, shutting and sealing it over him, so that he might not seduce the nations again till the thousand years were ended. After that he must be let loose for a little while. (20:1- 3)

The site of the final battle against the Anti-Christ is said to be Armageddon (Revelation 16:16), located in the ancient stronghold of Megiddo, roughly 15 miles south-east of Jerusalem.. The word Armageddon has now come to mean the final battle between the forces of Good and the forces of Evil.

Dajjalain system of Life

It is important to distinguish between Dajjal the individual, and Dajjal as a world-wide intellectual and social phenomenon based on materialism and atheism. The latter is manifested as the philosophical outlook that has taken shape during the last few centuries in Europe, as well as the culture and life-style based upon that Godless outlook. The system of life which is predominantly materialistic and which dominates the entire globe today is actually the "Dajjalian System" itself, whereas the greatest defender of that system will be Dajjal the individual.

As we have seen earlier, the innovations introduced by St. Paul in the original teachings of Prophet Isa (AS) had led to the genesis of a completely new and different religion. The highly irrational claim of Trinity ultimately resulted in the divorce between two natural allies, religion and reason. The conversion of Caesar Constantine in 313 C.E., and of the entire Roman Empire during the next hundred years or so, turned out to be the starting point for the establishment of Christian Theocracy in Europe. The huge vacuum created by the Pauline idea of abolition of the Mosaic law was then filled with the virtually unlimited authority of the Church, represented by the infallible Pope. During the Middle Ages the Church and the clergy ruled the masses with an iron hand, oppressing and exploiting them in the name of religion, while discouraging any inclination towards science or rationalism.

The Aristotelian system of cosmos, as adopted by Ptolemy, was already incorporated into the Christian theology. As a result, when Copernicus, Kepler, and Galileo opposed the Geocentric doctrine and proposed Heliocentric views based on their scientific observations, the Church condemned and vehemently opposed them as heretics, thus starting the unfortunate rivalry and rift between Science and Religion.

The scientific and rationalistic movement in Europe, therefore, came face to face with the powerful religious establishment of the Church. The latter used all its resources to halt this new wave of progress towards knowledge and learning, but succeeded only in producing among the masses a deep mistrust of all things connected with religion. The ruthlessly unfavorable attitude of the clergy caused a reactionary feeling of hatred against the Church, and then against the very idea of religion itself.

The development of science and philosophy in Europe, therefore, was forced to take place in an environment which was hostile to religion, and this hostility has since then permeated deep down into the very roots of Western thought. The world-view and civilization that grew out of this materialistic frame of mind is what we call the "Dajjalian System" of life. The hallmark of this system is a profound shift of emphasis — from God the Almighty to the material universe and laws of nature, from spiritual pursuits to sensual gratification, and from salvation in the life-after-death to material prosperity in this world.

Human beings have been endowed by Almighty Allah (swt) with two distinct sources of knowledge, that is, (a) information gathered by the senses and their interpretation by means of reason, intellect, and logic; along with (b) Revelation, in order to acquire knowledge of the ultimate realities and also the practical guidance for living a just, virtuous, and balanced life. However, the unfortunate shift of emphasis mentioned above resulted in a serious imbalance in the modern thinking process. Thus, while humanity has made an incredible amount of progress with regard to science and technology, we see that, correspondingly, religion and morality have undergone unprecedented decay and decline. As such, the Western civilization can be described as possessing only a single eye, epistemologically speaking. In other words, it has invested everything it had into a single source of knowledge — Reason and Science — while totally ignoring the other, equally important, source of knowledge — Revelation from the Heavens.

The system of life resulting from this materialistic mental attitude is characterized by a morbid preoccupation with collecting things and accumulating money. The corner stone of the Dajjalian System is the producer-consumer process, which is promoted as the ideal way of life. Highly sophisticated means are employed to convince the masses that they want newer and more expensive products, so that they can be made to work continuously in order to earn the money to pay for the goods and services they don't even need. The life blood of the Dajjalian System is usury, which is used to subjugate individuals as well as entire nations so that they can be controlled and manipulated by a financial aristocracy. The masses are encouraged to work hard, to enjoy their weekends, to uncritically digest whatever the media feeds them, and to invest all their time and energy in the pursuit of material well-being and sensual gratification. Humans are being reduced to the level of beasts. Endless consumption of products has become the dominant life-style of our times, and people have been made conditioned to measure each other on the basis of wealth and affluence, rather than character and morals. A whole entertainment industry has been created to keep the minds of the masses occupied whenever they are not working.

The entire system is geared so that the overwhelming majority is deprived of either the time or the energy to give any serious thought to the nature of existence, to the Creator, to the accountability in the Hereafter —

or to the exploiters. Dajjal the individual will represent the interests of those who are financially exploiting the whole world, against those who are being exploited. After the Armageddon, a Just Social Order will replace the present Dajjalian System, and there shall be no more exploitation.

The identity of Dajjal

The ultimate battle between the forces of Good and those of Evil requires a world that is highly polarized along ideological lines, and this has already started to take shape. The various Islamic movements throughout the world are clear proofs that more and more people are realizing the defects and inherent evils of the Dajjalian System, and are coming in contact with the true sources of knowledge, that is, the Holy Qur'an and the *Sunnah* of Prophet Muhammad (saw). The guardians of the status quo and the defenders of the New World Order, along with their agents and stooges, have already smelled the revolution that is taking shape in the form of Islamic Resurgence, and have started to try and suppress the idea whose time has come. The ultimate futility of their efforts is inevitable.

The Western and predominantly Christian countries of the world, as we have discussed above, are virtually being controlled by a very powerful Jewish minority — a recent accomplishment of which was the destruction of the military might of Iraq in the Gulf War. The next item on the Jewish agenda is the creation of Greater Israel, as well as the reconstruction of Solomon's Temple at the site of Al-Aqsa Mosque. It seems likely that the Jews would try to orchestrate another war between the West, mainly the United States, and the Arab Muslims, most probably on the pretext of dealing with the threat of Islamic fundamentalism.

Along with their sinister plan to gain control over the whole world through financial institutions — much of which has already been achieved — the Jews are also waiting for their Promised Messiah who would help them recapture the glory of David and Solomon. The Messiah was, in fact, none other than Prophet Isa (AS), but they opposed and rejected him and tried their very best to have him crucified, though he was miraculously saved by Almighty Allah (saw).

During the long series of imminent battles in the Middle East, Dajjal the individual would come forward — who is most probably going to be an orthodox and fundamentalist Jew claiming to be the Promised Messiah — and would lead his followers to the de facto creation of Greater Israel (which is supposed to include parts of Egypt, whole of Jordan and Syria, major portions of Iraq, southern Turkey, and northern Hijaz up to the holy city of Medinah). It will be at this crucial juncture of history that Almighty Allah (swt) will send the real Christ, with the mission of exterminating the Jews and their leader, Dajjal, the false prophet.

About Prophet Isa (as)

Although the exact nature of the ascension and reappearance of Prophet Isa (AS) is incomprehensible to us, and although these events are beyond the realm of normal human experience, they are by no means impossible. The rationalists among us tend to express serious doubts and lack of conviction about this authentic Islamic belief, but the fact is that our belief in the ascension and reappearance of Prophet Isa (AS) is based upon various indicators of the Holy Qur'an as well as explicit and unequivocal traditions of Prophet Muhammad (saw). The prevalence of materialistic thinking, especially under the influence of the now outdated Newtonian Physics, has caused many of our intellectuals to reject the possibility of miracles. But it must be kept in mind that a miracle, by definition, represents a breakdown in the usual physical laws of the universe, and a special creative feat of Almighty God is manifested from out of the ruins of that broken law. All natural laws have been established by Allah (swt), and He is able to suspend any of them for any period of time. He is Omnipotent, able to do all things.

It seems, on the basis of the predictions of Prophet Muhammad (saw), that both the Jews and the Arab Muslims will become the targets of Divine retribution in the final battles — but with a marked distinction. The condemned Children of Israel are going to be completely destroyed at the hands of their own prophet, Prophet Isa (AS), just as numerous other nations were removed from the face of the earth because they committed the crime of rejecting their respective messengers. On the other hand, the Muslims — especially the Arabs — will receive their share of punishment for turning away from the Holy Qur'an, but afterwards the survivors will be able to repent and mend their ways, paving the way for the beginning of the second phase of the domination of Islam.

From dishonor to Exhaltation

We had started our discussion with the assertion that the Muslim *Ummah* of today is a pathetic, miserable, and extremely humiliated group of people. The cause of this unfortunate state of affairs, as we have seen, is our own wrongdoing, our own sinful behavior, our own deviations from the straight path. It follows that the only way to escape from continuing Divine punishment and to regain our lost glory is to repent with the true spirit of repentance and to rectify our corrupted ways.

We the Muslims are the custodians of the last message of Allah (swt), representatives of the God- given system of life (*Deen al-Haq*), and intermediaries between Prophet Muhammad (saw) and the entire humanity. This means that it is our primary duty to struggle for the establishment of the perfect way of life, viz., Islam and its system of Social Justice, initially in a specific territory and then throughout the entire globe. According to the Holy Qur'an:

You are the best of community that has been raised up for the (guidance of) humanity; you (are therefore supposed to) enjoin the good, forbid the evil, and keep your own faith firm in God. (Aal-e- Imran 3:110)

Strive in the way of God with an endeavor worthy of Him. He has chosen you...in order that the Prophet be a witness against you, and you be witnesses against mankind. [TMQ Al-Hajj 22:78]

Thus We have appointed you a middle people (between the Prophet on one hand and the humanity on the other), so that you be witnesses against mankind, and the Messenger be a witness against you.

[TMQ Al- Baqarah 2:143]

Although this formidable but sacred duty of delivering the message of Islam to the entire mankind is the collective responsibility of the whole Muslim *Ummah*, God the Almighty does not burden any soul beyond its capacity, and therefore it is primarily the obligation of Arab Muslims, as the Holy Qur'an was revealed in their own language.

However, after the termination of Prophethood, Allah (swt) made a special arrangement to renew and revive the *Ummah* and her mission. Thus, after every three or four generations, i.e., after about every hundred years or so, a pious reformer appears among the Muslims to clarify and rejuvenate the original teachings of Islam. What is most significant in this respect is the fact that, during the first millennium of Islam, all of these reformers appeared almost exclusively in the Arab world. After the destruction of Baghdad in 1258, the academic and intellectual center of Islam started to shift towards the Indian subcontinent until, at the start of the second millennium, this part of the world became the main nucleus of Islamic reforms and revivalist movements. Thus, unusually great personalities have appeared here during the last four centuries, including Sheikh Ahmad Sirhindi (11th century *Hijrah*), Shah Waliyullah Delhvi (12th century), Sayyid Ahmad Barelvi (13th century), and more recently, Maulana Mehmood Hassan Deobandi, Allama Muhammad Iqbal, Maulana Muhammad Ilyas, and Maulana Abul A'la Maududi (14th century). Now the question arises: Are all these sincere efforts of the last four hundred years to go in vain? We believe the answer is an emphatic NO!

It seems that the burden of Arab Muslims has largely been shifted on to the shoulders of the Muslims belonging to the Indian subcontinent, and, especially after the claims and promises made during the movement for independence, the task of reviving Islam as a living force has now become the paramount responsibility of Pakistani Muslims. In view of the efforts undertaken during the last four centuries, this also appear to be their destiny.

Especially significant in connection with the role of Pakistani Muslims are the traditions of Prophet Muhammad (saw), which allude to the fact that our part of the world is going to be the starting point for the global Islamic domination; these traditions are given below:

(1) Ibn Maja (RA) has narrated on the authority of Abdullah Ibn Harith (RAA), that Prophet Muhammad (saw) is reported to have said that during the battles before the Doomsday: "Armies emerging from the East shall advance, and after conquering one country after another, they shall help and strengthen the authority of Mahdi."

(2) According to another tradition narrated by Imam Tirmidhi (RA), on the authority of Abu Huraira (RAA), Prophet Muhammad (saw) is reported to have said: "Black banners shall emerge from Khurasan (i.e., areas which are now included in Afghanistan and Pakistan), and no force will be able to stop them until they are inserted in Aelia (Jerusalem)."

These prophecies mean that there shall be in the future an Islamic State in the areas which today comprise Afghanistan and Pakistan (and perhaps also those which are included in Iran and Central Asia), so that during the final series of battles in the Middle East, armies from this part of the world will advance to fight against Dajjal under the leadership of Mahdi. A similar prophecy is also found in the Book of Revelation:

The sixth angel poured out his bowl on the Great River, the Euphrates; and its water was dried up to prepare a way for the kings from the east (16:12)

It must be understood that now, after the subjugation of the entire Arab world at the hands of the New World Order, it is only our part of the world that has the potential for standing up against the nefarious designs of the global power-brokers, and to resist the rising tides of the Jewish/Zionist hegemony. In view of the traditions of the Prophet (saw) given above, we are sure that the areas now included in Pakistan, Afghanistan, and Iran (the ancient Khurasan) have a very special significance in the Divine scheme.

The state of our Affairs

We believe — on the basis of the sayings of Prophet Muhammad (saw) and also because of the fact that the revivalist efforts of the last four hundred years have largely been concentrated in the Indian subcontinent — that the process of the global Islamic Revolution is going to start from our part of the world. Despite these high hopes and optimism, however, one must admit that the conditions are extremely depressing and almost totally hopeless at the moment.

As far as our own homeland is concerned, the history of the last half a century is clear proof of the truth that we have done everything in this country except what we were supposed to do in order to promote and substantiate its Islamic ideological character. We have followed every ideology except the one we should have. We have utterly and completely failed to live up to the claims and promises made during the struggle for independence in the 1940's.

During the years just prior to independence, we openly made solemn promises with Allah (swt) that Pakistan will represent a true Islamic State. This meant that we had recognized Islam not just as a system of beliefs and individual morality alone, but also as the only sources and criterion for our social, legal, cultural, economic, and political systems. *****The sense of a separate identity that became the basis of the idea of Muslim Nationhood was neither racial or linguistic in origin, nor based upon a common homeland, but it was founded upon our unique ideology, viz., our deep affiliation with and commitment to Islam.

The most crucial purpose behind the idea and struggle for Pakistan was Islamic renaissance and revival. As the ideologue of Pakistan Allama

Muhammad Iqbal explained in his famous presidential address at Allahbad, a Muslim state was meant to be "for Islam an opportunity to rid itself of the stamp that Arabian imperialism was forced to give it, to mobilize its law, its education, its culture, and to bring them into closer contact with its own original spirit and with the spirit of modern times."

This means that today we are living in a paradox. Although our country owes its existence to the Islamic ideology, we have so far failed to make any meaningful progress towards the implementation of that ideology. This also means that by refusing to honor our pledge with Almighty Allah (swt), we are ourselves responsible for inviting His anger and His retribution. The pathetic state of our affairs is, therefore, nothing but a manifestation of Divine punishment.

At an ideological level, our intelligentsia is almost completely in the favor of liberalism and permissiveness, a point of view based upon the materialistic and atheistic frame of mind which has been imported from the West. Thus, immodesty and licentiousness is being promoted in the name of entertainment and culture as the ideal standards of behavior for our young men and women. Morally, we are probably the worst group of people on the face of the earth. What to speak of Islamic ethics, we are even devoid of basic human values, as lying, cheating, and hypocrisy have become integral parts of our national character.

As for Islam itself, the majority of our uneducated and semi-educated population tend to treat their faith as only a set of dogmas which has nothing to do with a person's value structure. Among the educated classes, most are suffering from various degrees of atheism, skepticism, and agnosticism. A big chunk of our religious community is busy running after wealth and power, and the menace of sectarianism, which is continuously being fueled by them, has added another ominous dimension to the already worsening national chaos. And those who should help stop this madness — our political leaders — are themselves busy competing for their domination. The dangerously irresponsible and often illogical rhetoric that appears regularly in our national press is ample evidence that most of them don't care about anything but power. They make lovely promises of prosperity for the common man, but that poor fellow is often the last person on their list of beneficiaries.

The impending Doom

Under the prevailing circumstances, therefore, the possibility of an Islamic Revolution in Pakistan in the foreseeable future is almost non-existent. But to give up all hopes would be tantamount to giving in against the forces of disbelief. As a matter of fact, nothing is beyond the power of Almighty God, and it is only on the basis of our reliance on His succor that we are able to keep the hopes of a bright future alive.

Moreover, we also have in our minds a similar phase during the struggle of Prophet Muhammad (saw) when, after the death of his only apparent support — his uncle Abu Talib — in the 10th year of Prophethood, the chances of an Islamic Revolution in Arabia appeared thin and bleak. It could have been assumed that the leaders of Quraysh would kill the Prophet and thereby terminate the whole movement. Desperate to find a new base, Prophet Muhammad (saw) went to Ta'if, but was violently rejected there and forced out of the town. Returning to Makkah, he realized that he would be immediately killed upon entering the city, and was therefore forced to ask for the protection of Mut'im Ibn Adi. The gentleman — who never embraced Islam — arrived at the outskirts of Makkah, and, together with his six armed sons, escorted Prophet Muhammad (saw) to the city, announcing his protection. Even after these utterly hopeless conditions, however, the Islamic movement not only survived, but the greatest revolution of all times was achieved in the Arabian Peninsula within the next ten years.

Thus, even though the present conditions in Pakistan are extremely discouraging — especially in relation to the growing influence of Washington, which has a particular antipathy towards Islamic fundamentalism and revivalism — we are still hopeful that our country and the adjoining areas would form, sometime in the very near future, a genuine Islamic State. As for the question "When shall that be?" the following answers can be quoted from the Holy Qur'an:

They surely take it to be far away, but We see it very near!

[TMQ Al-Ma'arij 70:6,7]

and

Say: "I do not know if what is promised to you is near, or if my Lord will prolong its term." [TMQ Al-Jinn 72:25]

However, there are two distinct possibilities for our immediate future: Either we will turn towards Allah (swt) in repentance, in which case the impending punishment shall hopefully be revoked, or we will continue to sink even deeper into sinfulness, in which case — and it is not easy to face these bitter realities — we might suffer a really major disaster, and only then shall we wake up from our slumber. The choice is ours; though, unfortunately, we have so far been opting for the latter.

Aldous Huxley has said that the most important of all the lessons that history has to teach is that men do not learn very much from the lessons of history. The events of the last four thousand years, as narrated very briefly in these pages, clearly show how God the Almighty punishes His "beloved" people whenever they transgress His commands. In this context, Pakistani Muslims are already feeling the pangs of minor punishments from Allah (swt), and, unless we repent, a major episode of Divine retribution seems imminent, the signs of which are already in the air. In the words of Jesus Christ, "Already the ax is laid to the roots of the trees; and every tree that fails to produce good fruit is cut and thrown on the fire" (Luke 3:9).

Repentance: The only way to Salvation

What needs to be done, therefore, if we are to escape from the impending catastrophe, is to turn towards Allah (swt), repent truly, and make a solemn vow to practice Islam in its totality.

The starting point of collective repentance of a nation is repentance by its individual members. This must include a real feeling of regret, a firm resolve never to repeat the sins, followed by actual change in behavior, and, in the case of any violation of the rights of other human beings, an appropriate compensation or asking for forgiveness from the aggrieved party. This individual repentance, if performed with its true spirit, does guarantee forgiveness from Almighty Allah (swt) in the Hereafter. It does not mean, however, that the individual will escape any collective Divine punishment that might befall his nation (Al-Qur'an Al- Anfaal 8:25), except in the case when he had used all available resources and had tried his utmost to persuade others to give up their sinful practices (Al-Qur'an Al-A'raaf 7:165).

The desired state of collective repentance can be achieved only when first of all a considerable number of individuals would repent and mend their ways; then they unite themselves into a cohesive force and change the main trend of the society by their exhortation and persuasion, their enjoining the good and forbidding the evil, leading to a revolution in thought as well as behavior. And then, in order to change the whole politico-socio-economic setup, a popular resistance movement would have to be launched, which will bring about the desired transformation through a non-violent revolutionary struggle. At the same time, a strong nucleus of *Iman* or true faith has to be created within the educated classes, especially among the intelligentsia, which would act as a center for rekindling the light of

Iman throughout the whole society, and thus generate an intellectual base and popular support for the revolutionary struggle The establishment of the Islamic System of Social Justice would then represent our collective repentance.

Epilogue

Prophet Muhammad (saw) has prophesied that a time would come when the Muslims, though great in number, would be as weak and ineffective as the scum on the surface of flood waters.

One can hardly doubt that we are living in that age. Our miserable state of existence, as we have seen, is the direct result of our own deeds: Our turning away from the guidance of the Holy Qur'an and the way of Prophet Muhammad (saw). Fortunately, our salvation in the Hereafter and our prosperity, honor, and domination in this world are a matter of choice rather than luck.

We have been suffering from the ill effects of our sins for too long. Has the time not yet come for the hearts of the believers to be moved and soften? Or are we waiting for The Punishment to appear right before our eyes?

It's time to wake up; it is also the time to act.

www.ingramcontent.com/pod-product-compliance
Lightning Source LLC
Chambersburg PA
CBHW062141160726
48282CB00027B/895
* 9 7 8 9 3 9 4 8 3 4 5 7 6 *